WHAT IS YOUR WHY?

Behind The Drive

Josias Jean Pierre

Life Chronicles Publishing

ISBN- 978-1-950649-25-9

Editor Life Chronicles Publishing

Cover Design: Life Chronicles Publishing

Life Chronicles Publishing Copyright © 2019

lifechroniclespublishing.com

TABLE OF CONTENTS:

CHAPTER ONE

PURPOSE

Everything that happens in this world happens with a purpose. The family we were born in, the conditions we were born with, the obstacles we go through in life, all have a meaning. We may not know the reasons tragedies and circumstances occur, but one thing is for sure, we don't have to understand it at all. Our purpose in life is not about how big our circle is and how popular we become in our lives. However, it's about the legacy we leave behind.

When we understand our purpose for living, then we will become aware of the value and importance of the influence of our calling. Many individuals know what they want to be, but many people don't envision themselves moving towards their intended goals. Jeremiah 29:11 says, *"For I know the plans I have for you says the Lord, plans to prosper you and not harm you, plans to give you hope and a future."*

Even before we were pushed out of the womb of our mothers, God already had our futures mapped out. I remember as a young child growing up, I never quite understood the why behind a J.O.B (Just Over Broke) I never quite understood why we said, "America is the land of opportunity." Still, everybody has a job that can never really give them what they need to fulfill their destiny on this earth. I never quite understood why my mother had to work two jobs to provide for her kids and why she was working so hard for a paycheck that she would have to work all over again to make ends meet. I didn't see the purpose of sweating to make someone else's dream become a reality, only to realize the job cannot fulfill our dreams. I remember it was 8th grade (2006), and I was reflecting on the purpose of why I was here. I knew there was something more than just working 9-5, because something in me told me, this wasn't it. I did everything I could to acquire new skills to make a better life for myself. I did everything I could to figure out my "why" in life.

In the middle of February 2007, I found my "why" and purpose. I remember watching Martin Luther King Jr. and he was giving his, *"I Have A Dream"* speech. There was something about that speech that triggered me to listen and absorb what he was saying. MLK said he had a dream, and that dream was something that was revealed to him, and no matter what, he kept that dream present. It is your "why" that will drive you to keep on going even when life hits rock bottom. It will help you bounce back even when it might seem hard to jump back up. Our purpose in life is to leave a legacy behind that can carry on from generation to generation.

What we do with our experiences will dictate how people remember us when we are gone. MLK has a legacy that is still alive because he seen what he was speaking. What is your why? Is it big enough to push even if nobody stands with you? Is your "why" big enough to keep you when trials and tribulations come to stop you?

As a young boy with a diagnosis of epilepsy, I was told that I would never be able to achieve as much as others. I was told to stop believing in my dreams, but they never knew the purpose that lived in me. I remember being in class in February of 2007. I was writing a paper on what I wanted to become. I kept writing it and writing it. While writing, I also kept speaking my dreams into existence. Every time I spoke it, I felt I was one step closer to doing that which I believed I could do. It did not matter what people said; I knew I was heading in the right direction. This is the affirmation I spoke, "I, Josias Jean-Pierre, will be an inspirational speaker and influence communities and schools, teaching people the importance of education and the importance of possessing healthy thoughts. I will be an advocate for kids with disabilities and show them that they are not accidents; they are here for a purpose." These words sealed my destiny. People laughed at me because they thought it was impossible; others told me to stop dreaming because there was no way a special-needs kid could accomplish anything like that. Like the words of Bruno Mars, *"If you don't believe me, just watch!"* This dream that I had turned into a deep conviction that caused me to believe I would do it. No matter what anybody said, I knew I would step into the next big thing. I was so excited that I went home and shared it with my older brother Jephtey Jean-Pierre.

At the age of seventeen (senior year), I got booked to speak at a national conference called the American School Health Association (ASHA) in Kansas City, Missouri. I spoke about the importance of education and advocating for children with disabilities. In May of 2011, I was the keynote speaker for the twentieth anniversary for the City of Sea-Tac in WA.

When we know our purpose, we will be cautious about who is trying to enter and influence our lives. Our lives are precious, and if we are not aware that we are created for a purpose, we will never be able to know *the why behind the drive*. We can move around all we want, but if there's no drive behind our journey, then it becomes pointless. We should know why we are doing whatever we choose to do. Purpose says, "I am doing it for a bigger reason and a bigger cause." This is not just about me, but this is about what will be left behind. Purpose says, if nobody else stands with me, I am going to stand even if it means I'm alone. What is your purpose? What is it that makes you tick to the point where you want more? What is it that motivates you to say, *I have to do something different because change starts with me?* I had to let some people go because they were hindering me from going to where I was going.

God had a purpose for sending his only begotten son to die for us (John 3:16). God will never do anything that doesn't have meaning and value. God knew that each of us was going to make a mistake and fall, but we are valuable to Him. He did not send his son to the world to condemn the world, but that the world be saved through him (John 3:17). Like my brother would say, *"There's nothing you can do to make God stop loving you, and there's nothing you can do to make God regret that he died for you."* Jephtey Jean-Pierre. His plans will not change even if you feel a certain way.

So many of us have let the pain of our past determine our lives. You are not your past experiences, so don't let anyone tell you that you can't become stronger, wiser, and better because of what you went through. You didn't go through what you went through for no reason. As a matter of fact, you went through what you went through because it's a part of the process for you to walk into your destiny and greatness. What you have gone through is the story you have to share with others who may be currently experiencing what you have gone through.

I never quite understood why my father told my brothers and me at a young age to never call him dad, he's not our dad. It was hard for me to comprehend how a parent could neglect and reject his own sons, leaving them emotionally wounded. See, I was so hurt because of his actions that I started hurting other people. Hurting people, hurt people. I was so hurt that my pain blinded me to see the pain I was causing everyone else. I started to act out with violent behaviors and drama as a cry for help. While I was in pain, I always told myself there was a reason why I was going through this. I was losing friends left and right because I was afraid to get the help I needed. It wasn't until I was coming to the end of my sophomore year that I attended a sling-shot all city youth conference in Tukwila WA. The theme was, *Defeating the Giants in our Lives that Could Hold us Back from Moving Forward.*

I remember asking God to deliver me from this pain that I was carrying that day at the conference. I remember walking away, feeling free from the bondage of hatred. The moment I chose to let go of the pain that was holding me back, I was able to walk with my chin high and move forward to the next level in life. It wasn't an immediate awareness; it took time for me to understand.

I remember being in college, and there was a job offer to work at a camp called Camp Berachah, located in Black Diamond, WA, (now known as Black Diamond Camp). There were two ladies talking about how God was using them for ministry as camp counselors. For a long time, I asked God to explain why I was allowed to be a part of this moment. I found out that these ladies were actually recruiting for counselors, and I immediately applied to be a camp counselor without even knowing the details. I was excited about this opportunity for God to use me, and I thought I was prepared to do His work.

However, there was a spiritual battle waiting for me, and I almost threw in the towel. Kids were almost sent home because of bad behavior, and I was so upset because I didn't know how to reach them. Around the 3rd day, something in me told me to talk about the pain of a father and how God delivered me. I said to them that God is a father to the fatherless, and he is a hope to the hopeless. All of a sudden, these campers started crying because they never felt the love of a father. Our devotion was so powerful that the whole atmosphere changed, and you knew it was God moving right in the midst of it all. People were starting to see a significant change from my campers. They came there not wanting to worship, but then that changed to them wanting to worship God. They were hungry to know more about His word. All of my campers grew up without fathers, and before the camp was over, they all had a personal relationship with God and accepted the Lord as their personal savior. At that moment, I realized why I went through what I did with my father, to be a help to others who were hurting and broken from being fatherless. Three of my campers told me that, if God hadn't moved in their lives, they would have committed suicide. One of them stated that they go to camp every year, just going through the motions as if they enjoyed camp but they didn't. The camper told me that they never had an experience like they had in devotion. At the moment, I literally cried because these kids who were the most painful kids to deal with were beginning to believe again. I realized the "why" behind the struggle of being fatherless for 15 years.

Your story can restore hope to the hopeless and joy to those who have lost their joy. You may not understand the puzzle piece to the struggle that you may have endured, but know this: you don't have to understand one bit of it. The puzzle piece of your life is not in the hands of the world but it's in the hands of God. Sometimes, God has to break us apart to put us back together again so we can be made stronger, wiser and better.

Many of us want to step into greatness but we don't want to go through the process of being broken and being put back together. In order to walk into your purpose, there is a process that will take place. Everyone was born for a great commission and that commission is what will dispatch us to walk into our destiny. To know your purpose, you must understand your pain.

A familiar story that we may have heard is the story of Job. See, Job lost everything and he didn't quite know what was going on and why things were happening the way they were happening. Chaos was his test. When we experience our Job moments, we could become angry and question God; we could even blame the devil. What we have to understand is that even though God let Satan do what he wanted to do with Job, but he could not touch a finger on his body. Even though he didn't understand what was going on, he didn't let the problem dictate the belief he had in God. Throughout the story of Job, one thing we can see is, after the storm was over, a blessing came his way. In the beginning, Job was already blessed, but in the latter part of Job's life, he was more blessed. In Job 42:12 it says, *"The LORD blessed the latter part of Job's life more than the former part. He had fourteen thousand sheep, six thousand camels, a thousand yoke of oxen and a thousand donkeys."* What was lost has been restored, and when God restores things, he restores in ways that we can't even fathom or even imagine.

In life, we all will go through some storms and those storms are not there to punish you, but to build you up and push you towards the next level. The enemy (Satan) will try to do what he can in his might and power to make you believe that God is not with you during trials. When you look at your circumstances with a lens of the carnal, it will be hard for you to believe that you can conquer what may seem like it's impossible to conquer. See your trial the way God sees it. What does that mean? Know that God will bring you through. You will let the enemy know that a breakthrough is on the way for you! You will be able to speak to the mountains of your life and demand it to flee. In the book of Matthew, it tells us that if we have faith as small as a mustard seed, we can say to the mountain to move from here or there, and it will move. Nothing will be impossible for us (Matthew 17:20). In this verse, we would have thought it was talking about a physical mountain. However, it was speaking about the storms and mountains of our lives that we may have to endure.

We will know ourselves by our trials and tribulations. We can't become better, stronger, and wiser if we are staying in a place of being comfortable. When you are comfortable, you will never grow and when you don't grow, you stay stagnant.

When you're comfortable, you're not living out your full potential; when you are not living out your full potential, you're wasting life and your time. There's a world that is dying that needs the true you, who God created you to be. There's a world that is aching, desperate and in need of hope. What if you are the only hope that they can see? Please don't sit on your calling because it's your calling that will leave an impact. We are needed in a time like this, where chaos is happening and it seems like brokenness and hopelessness is disturbing our communities, schools, and jobs. We are needed to be the agents of change in a time like this.

Don't wait for someone else to do the work. God has called you to be that superwoman or superman in someone's life. The keys of change are in your hands from the moment you were born. The question is, what are you doing with those keys? What are you doing every day to better help the folks around you? What is your why? Is your why big enough to sustain you, no matter how tough it gets, or how hard the roadblock is, or who comes with you? This is the question we have to ask ourselves every time.

CHAPTER TWO

THE GOAL SETTERS

Just because you have goals does not mean that you know your purpose. Having goals is great! However, attaining those goals are the key. Here are two types people in life: those who are goal setters and those who are goal hitters. I will go over them below.

Have you ever met someone who makes goals for themselves but never achieves them? They forget about the original goal but then proceed to make another goal. Have you ever met someone who talks big and has many aspirations, but never really hit their targets? The goal setter is the individual who can set goals and make them sound good but knows deep inside they don't believe they can achieve them. This individual is a big talker but there's not much action taken on their part. The goal setter is the individual who is like a salesperson selling a product to get a commission, however, they don't believe that they are a good salesperson.

There are three hundred and sixty-five days in a year, and for many of us, every year, we make a New Year resolution that we never follow through with. We are so good at talking about our resolutions, and not achieving results. Whatever you want to see changed in your life, circumstances, communities, and your workplace don't wait until December 31st to start to do something about it. Just do it right now in the moment. We need to become the people of now instead of the people of tomorrow. Tomorrow is never promised, and when we procrastinate, we put off what really matters to us. Goal setters are the ones that can make goals and never achieve them because they can't see themselves there, resulting in failure and inconsistency. When you make goals without a plan, it's not a goal it's just a wish. In everything that we do, we must have a plan. Your "why" can't manifest if you don't know how to make it manifest. If your dream is to become a doctor, lawyer, psychologist, psychiatrist, etc.; what steps are you taking to achieve your dreams?

There's an individual I know by the name of Bob. Bob was the dude in college that people thought was going to be a big shot in life because he had many goals. He would make goals left and right and he carried himself in a way where you would have believed that he achieved each one of the goals. However, I knew Bob and I knew he wasn't hitting his targets; I knew that he was struggling big time with his goals. Bob was the 4.0 student that everyone went to for assistance with classwork. School was something that Bob loved and he was educated and could past a test even if he was not in the class. You may know someone like that. But what Bob couldn't do was envision himself in the field he wanted. He was told he should be a counselor because he gave good advice and he should work with folks who were struggling with drugs and alcohol. Bob allowed them to influence him and decided to go for it.

One time after graduating from college, Bob and I went out to eat and he found out that I published my first book. We met up and the first thing I said to Bob was, "Dang man, how are you doing? Mr. 4.0 student graduated number one in the class with honors left and right." Before he even let me finish, he goes:

"J, I got to tell you something." He was upset and had a look of frustration.

"What's going on?" I asked him.

"I can't see myself as a counselor; I did it for someone else; I didn't do it for me." He responded. "Truth to be told, I knew I didn't want to go into this field but I didn't want to hurt others who saw something in me that I couldn't see in myself. I am struggling and I don't know what to do from here. And since you are a motivational speaker, I want to hear some ideas from you."

I remember telling Bob, "I can't motivate you solely, you have to want this for yourself. If you don't have some self-motivation, then others can't motivate you at all.

Before there's motivation, there's inspiration, and when inspiration comes, you will be motivated because you got inspired. Just because you have a goal, it doesn't mean that you have plan."

"What do you mean?" He responds.

"You are a goal setter but not a goal hitter. In whatever you do, you do it well but when the task gets done you don't have a plan." I took a breath, then I told him, "A goal without a plan is just a wish, and you can wish all you want, but if you don't see it becoming real to you, then your wish and your goal is just a waste."

Bob knew how much I cared for him and knew that I wouldn't hold anything back so, when he came and sat with me, he knew what he was doing. Bob then asked me what he should do. My response was, to believe.

"You have to believe that you can achieve what you want. Write things on paper and speak them into existence and make sure when you are speaking it into existence, you're speaking it with confidence and belief. I let Bob know that he had to change his circle of influence or his circle of Influence would change him.

Then, Bob looked at me and said, "You mean to tell me I have to write things on paper and speak it into existence? Can I just speak into existence without writing anything?"

I let Bob know he could speak it into existence, but it wouldn't be clear to him at all until he started writing it on paper. "The more you write it, the clearer it becomes; and the clearer it comes, that's when you will eventually see it." After our meeting, he said he would go and do that process and would follow up with me to give an update. Around mid-July of 2017, Bob and I had dinner again and caught up.

Today, Bob is a family man, he runs a mentor group, developing and empowering youth. While he was sharing his update with me, the one question I asked him was, "What is your why?" He stated his why from his heart with boldness and confidence. When you know your why, you will be hungry to see it manifest. Once it manifests, you will realize that trials, tribulations, heartaches, and pain are all part of the process to step into your purpose.

We have to understand that, if we don't believe it, we will never achieve it. And if we don't see it, we will never reach it. And if we don't reach it, then we are going around in circles expecting different results. So many of us have goals but don't have a plan. We don't make plans to fail. However, we fail because we don't plan. The number one reason why people repeat the same cycle is because they have no plan.

Before a house can be built, it has to have a solid foundation or else everything will crumble, and you'll have to start from the beginning over again. It's the same as life.

Many of us feel like we need to be approved or someone needs to give us permission to do what we want to do. Goal setters tend to be the ones that talk about their goals but will choose to procrastinate. There are many examples that I can go over that can explain the wasted life, but, I believe, these three will nail it home for us before we get to the 2nd part of the goal setters.

"Good Enough" Has Become The New Standard

One thing we have to understand in this life is, we were not born to do the ordinary. We are born to do the extraordinary. When you decide to say good enough is my new standard, you are limiting yourself from your full potential and purpose. Good enough should never become your standard, and when that does become your standard, you're choosing an ordinary life. To grow, we must be okay with being uncomfortable, growth demands it.

Goal setters are good at being good enough. They are good with words, but not good with follow-through. Are you content with where you're at? Are you satisfied with just being good enough? Are you content with the results you're reaping? Are you content with the legacy that you might leave behind? And if you say no to any of these, then what are you willing to do about it? If you say no to any of these, are you ready to change the standards that you have set for yourself? If your response was a yes, why is it a yes? When you say you're content with being good enough, you're saying that you accept that you did good enough work so that you can pass. For some of us, we will take a "good enough" lifestyle. Comfortability says, I am only going to do what I am comfortable with, and I am okay if I only push out mediocre results. Being uncomfortable means there's more to this, and I am going to push to win even if it's going to hurt.

I remember being asked to speak at the WA State, *"Trio Civic Leadership Conference,"* the theme of the conference was called "Igniting Your Passion in Leadership." This was a conference that Junior Colleges, Universities, and High Schools came out to be equipped and inspired to become leaders of today. At this conference, I did a workshop called *"The Power Of I."* In this workshop, I talked about the Inner-self and the power that is within. I hosted one workshop at two different times, I asked the attendees to explain their passions and what they are doing to fulfill their dreams. One thing I found out was that the majority of the students in the first session said that they were not focused on their passions at the moment, and they were just doing enough to get by in life. I had to make sure I heard it correctly, and I repeated what they said to them. Then, I asked them to explain what getting by means. One student said, "You know just doing mediocre work or getting an F just to pass. I heard other students say the same thing and they were proud of it. I gave them an example of my explanation for the grading system.

A= Employee of the Year
B= Employee of the Month
C= Employee of the Week
F= You just got fired.

I went on and asked the students if an employer had to see their transcript to determine their employment, what would they see. Immediately, pens dropped, and the students were getting teary-eyed because, when they understood how I broke down A-F, they knew that they were not doing enough to be the employee of the month or year. I asked the students, "What results does the employer see? Do you want them to see you as the student who pushes out C's and F's work, or do you want them to see you as the student who pushes out A's and B's?" All of them said A's and B's, and I told them if they wanted that, then good enough and being ordinary are not an option.

Whatever you do, you have to give 100% even if it means you're standing alone. In the second session, we talked about the power within and what their passion was. The majority of the students knew their passion, but they stated that they were too young to focus on their ideas, and just wanted to enjoy life while they could. Tomorrow is never promised, and if you can't work on your passion now, you will never work on your passion at all. Good-enough work will only get you by, but unleashing that power within can get you through life. Don't think you are too young to be used and don't think you are too young to ignite that passion within you. It's the passion within that will influence you and open doors that you didn't think will open. Please don't sit on what is inside of you because that thing breathing inside of you can unleash your full potential. Another way we can waste our life is by excuses.

You Always Have A Reason Not To Take Action

In life, we will find ways to get out of things, so we don't have to do them. The more excuses you bring, the more moments you will miss to make things better in life. I remember my communications 101 teacher in college, Laura Manning. Now, Mrs. Manning was the type of teacher who everybody loved, and at the same time was very strict. One thing that she has always said was, *"Don't give me excuses, give me solutions."* She didn't care about what happened; she cared about what we were going to do about it. That's the same with life. It doesn't matter what happens; however, it does matter what you are going to do about it. In life, we have to be people of solutions and not people of excuses. You can't become who you want to be with a mentality of excuses. You need to be willing to fight for what you want. Stand up for what you believe in.

If we want better for ourselves and our kids, we must be willing to sacrifice our excuses. Have you ever met someone who has an excuse for everything? Like literally everything... you tell them to do this and that, and they have an excuse for it right then. You bring them an opportunity to improve themselves, then they automatically come back saying it's not real, it's not true, or that can't happen. We cannot live life by sight alone; we must have faith that we will always grow, prosper, and prevail. Someone who lives by sight says, "I have to see it to believe it, and if I don't see it, then it's not real." Someone who lives life by faith says, "I may not be able to see it, but if I keep on believing, then I shall see it come to pass. I may not see it in this moment or this present hour, but if I keep manifesting, it shall come to pass." Sad to say, many of us have more excuses than we have solutions, and we wonder why our goals will never flourish because we keep producing albums of excuses. Lastly, let's deal with past hurts.

Past Hurts

Past hurts kill many of us because we are unwilling to deal with them. Toxic relationships, friendships, unforgiveness, holding a grudge for something that was done long ago is unhealthy. It is impossible to walk into your why when you are walking with hurt from the past. All of us are born limitless, and when we carry wounds of the past, those wounds cause us to have limitations we don't recognize. Understand that the pain of your past can get you to the point of self-doubt and self-hatred because it hasn't been dealt with. We live in a world that tells us not to show any fear, and if you do show fear or any emotions, then you are not a strong human being. The world doesn't get to define who you are. And don't let the world tell you how you should live your life from day to day. Understand that you were made in an image of God and not an image of man. Know that, when you are hurting and you're not willing to deal with your pain, that pain will grow. Over time, instead of you living life, the pain of your past will live your life. The best way to walk free from the pain of the past is to forgive. Marianne Willamson once said, "Unforgiveness is like drinking poison yourself and waiting for the other person to die." The pain over the years can bind you and keep you stuck in bondage. You will spread the hurt you feel to others; you may not realize that you are hurting others.

I remember being in school, and to graduate we had to take a test called "WASL" (Washington Assessment for Students Learning). This was a state test that everyone had to take to graduate out of high school. If you didn't pass, you wouldn't graduate. For some people, this test was painful because it would show what was retained. I remember the day when the results came back, and the school counselor said that I passed, and I would be graduating and getting my diploma. I was stoked and ready to step into the next chapter of my life to see what the next level had in store for me. This test was hard for some. However, just because it was painful, it didn't mean that we should dwell on the pain of the test. The same applies in life.

The pain you are holding onto are like chains that refuse to break; they can become strongholds in your life. No matter how hard life gets, it's not worth looking back. Stay on course and fight the good fight because when you are focused, you are on the right track. The acronym of 'PAST' is this:

Passing
Already
Standardized
Test.

Everything you have gone through is building you up for your purpose, and every roadblock you have faced is just preparing you for impact. Don't look at what you are going through as a roadblock, but look at what you are going through as if it's getting you ready for greatness. Behind every mess, there's a message, and behind every test, there's a testimony. Your story is needed somewhere, and someone needs to hear how you overcame what you've gone through. Let what you go through become a footprint of impact instead of regrets. Let what you go through become a footprint of blessings instead of a footprint of curses. What does that mean? The problem is never what we are going through; however, it's more of how we respond to what we go through. What we go through has never been intended to kill us, but it's there to build us up. The storms in life are not here to punish us, their purpose is to make us stronger, wiser, and better. How you respond to what you are going through can shape the years ahead of you and your legacy.

Goal Setters That Are Goal Hitters

The second type of people are the people who are not only goal setters but are also goal hitters. These people take action and plan, even if it means nobody believes in their plan. These are the type of people who go beyond their comfort zone and who won't settle for anything less. They don't just make a plan to make a plan. They make a plan and put it in writing, and their words become a conviction, and that conviction turns into belief. They eventually walk into that plan. Understand that everything in life is an investment, but we shouldn't invest in everything. To become goal hitters, I believe ten things need to happen.

1. Words That Are Spoken

The most powerful weapons that we, as humans, carry in life is our tongues, it is the most powerful. The words that we tend to speak over our lives have so much power that they can break us, build us, or even kill us. The words that we choose to speak into each other's lives can turn into a belief, and that belief can destroy who we are or build us up. What you decide to speak in life has the power to manifest in your life. We have to understand that our tongue plays a role. If you are not speaking positive affirmations over your life, then what you are doing is affirming negative results.

What are you speaking over your life today? When you wake up, and you look in the mirror, what are some of the words you are telling yourself? What are you speaking into the atmosphere that can become a stumbling block in your life? Music can also influence your life's outcomes. If the music is not empowering you, building you, and strengthening you, then it's probably a hindrance. You might say that makes no sense. There's a phrase that states you are what you eat. If you consume garbage, then what you will produce is going to be garbage. You can't expect to create greatness with a garbage mentality. You can't expect to walk into full purpose with a negative attitude. When it comes to music, we have to understand what we listen to can change our lives.

We have to change the words we speak, manifest, download, and predict over our lives. To become the man or woman of courage, we have to be able to become people who bounce back. There are three things we have to understand when we talk about words that can affect our "why."

1. Words spoken will determine your belief.
2. Words spoken will determine your circle of influence.
3. Words spoken will determine your lifestyle.

When you plant words, they will turn into beliefs. Make sure that what you are listening to and what you are speaking over your life is bringing positive fruit and not rotten fruit. To activate the "why" in your life, you have to be able to speak words that will bring out the best in you. Many times, we let the tragedies of life move us towards defeat instead of victory. You can't be your best with a mentality that is defeated. To become a goal setter and a goal hitter, your words have to change so you can break what may seem like impossible obstacles.

2. Stop Procrastinating on The Goals That Matter To You

We have become people of procrastination. We want results right now but don't want to do the work. It's time to get serious about reaching your goals. You won't get the results you want by procrastination. Some of us procrastinate and push things off to the last minute. We are good at saying, "I will do it later," and when later comes, it never happens. We need to condition our minds to become people of now and not people of later. Every minute you procrastinate about the things you say matter to you, is a minute you have missed impacting someone else. Tomorrow is never promised, and we need to stop thinking and believing that tomorrow is an option. They're two choices in life, accept conditions as they are or take the responsibility and change them; which one of those options is a reflection of your life. When you choose to accept the conditions of life, you are saying that you are content with where you are. Procrastination should never be an option.

The more you choose to procrastinate, the more you allow the fire inside of you to die. We all have something that we are passionate about and something that we want to see change in our communities, lives, and schools. We need to take action right now, people. When we keep taking breaks and pauses these moment will eventually lose what was once called, our passion.

Pushing through
All
Situations
So
I can
Overcome
Now

The acronym that I made for Passion is "Pushing Through All Situations So I can Overcome Now." The word *now* does not mean it's going to happen instantly, but it means "I am going to start the process. I am going to see a change in time." Understand that it is through your trials and tribulations that endurance is built. The hurts of life will develop your passion. Your passion is your calling, and one thing about callings is, once you are called, the calling can't be taken away. I never knew I was called to be a light to young brothers and sisters until I was going through some misery of my own. When the storm was over, there was a passion that was birthed inside of me. It was there all along. Don't procrastinate on what you say matters to you. The fact that it matters to you should be a reason why you don't make procrastination an option.

3. Being Indecisive About What You Want

Goal setters that are goal hitters can't be indecisive about what they want. You will never leave where you are now until you decide where you want to be. When you do know where you would rather be, for it to become possible, you have to make it plain on paper. Goal setters that are goal hitters make sure they can see themselves there. The moment they see themselves, is the moment that will drive them to their destiny. You can't be a goal setter and a goal hitter if you can't see yourself in that position.

We have been told to close our eyes and imagine our dream house and dream car; imagination alone will not make it happen for you. The first step that we have to take is putting your goals on paper. I remember being a young kid, and I kept on writing my vision on paper. The more I wrote it, the more I declared it, and the more I said it, the more it became clear for me. As I prospered, those around me began to as well. You can't leave where you are without having a plan of where you are going. In the book of Habakuk 2:2, we see in this chapter that the Lord told Habakuk to write down the revelation so it could be plain and other folks who saw it could run with it. Proclaim what we want with words of faith and not words of doubt.

Sometimes, we repeat the same levels of life because of the uncertainty that we attach to our goals, dreams, and visions. Doubt is like a boomerang; no matter how far it goes, it comes back to the same spot. You will repeat the same life levels/circumstances because of doubt. When we talk about our "why," indecisiveness should not be an option.

A lot of times, when we don't know what we want, we will settle for anything that may look good. Not everything that looks good is perfect. And not everything that may look beneficial is beneficial in the long run. One of my favorite quotes is from Malcolm X., "A man who stands for nothing will fall for anything." What are you willing to stand for? Are you ready to stand alone for it?

Make sure you know what you want, or else the world will show you what you want based on what tempts you.

4. Letting The Opinions of Others Affect Your Life.

We live in a world where there are mixed messages, and we let the opinions of others affect our lives. To be goal hitters and goal setters, we cannot let people's opinions dictate what we do. You have the final say about what you want in life.

Earlier, I mentioned how our tongue is the most powerful weapon that we as humans carry. When we allow opinions of others in our lives, it's no longer what we believe, but what they believe. What others have said about you are opinions, but what you have said about yourself are facts. For some of us, we have heard the views of others who told us we are stupid, up to no good, can't become anything, will never become great, etc. While we hear these words, we also think we are great, we can become anything and we are not stupid. Don't listen to those words of destruction. If the words of your peers are not building you up and pushing you, then you need some new peers. You reap what you sow, so be careful with what is being sowed.

When we live a life based on messages from the media, peers, and family members, what we are doing is silencing our voice and believing that our voice has no value, no power, or an effect of doing anything. We can hinder ourselves from seeing the clear vision of our purpose. Negativity wasn't a piece of your puzzle when you were created, so don't let negativity be a piece of your puzzle when you try to blossom into greatness. Doubt wasn't a piece of your puzzle when you were pushed out to do great work, so don't let doubt become a puzzle piece. There's a difference between opinions and facts, and if we can't tell the difference between a lie and the truth, then what will happen is that we will live a life based on lies.

Anything negative should not be a part of who you are, and everything that is uplifting should be a part of who you are. What drives people is positivity. What is it that you're feeding yourself every day? What are some of the words influencing your life? Change your words, and you can change your world. When your words change, your thoughts change, and when your thoughts change, your actions change, and when your actions change, that's when you will walk undefeated.

Many of us have felt like we aren't anything because of the world that continuously says who we are or what we should be. Some of these messages we see through social media, music, ads, commercials, and almost everywhere around us, we tend to believe them. One thing that we have to understand is that the voices of others will never have power over your voice unless you let it have power.

There is someone on the inside of you that is hungry to be released into the public. That someone is craving for the real you to come out and be authentic. Every one of us has a desire that is burning on the inside, but we don't want to be rejected. We want to be accepted. To blossom into a goal setter that is a goal hitter, you have to make a decision to be real with yourself. It's not about what they say, but it's about what *you* say. You don't need anybody's permission to walk into the best you that God created you to be. The moment you were put in this world, you were already great!

Your birth makes you great! It is your key to becoming extraordinary. This world doesn't need duplicates; it needs originals. Show the world the real you. Make sure what you are downloading into your life (including the music you listen to) is building you up and not tearing you apart.

5. The Shame of Past Failures

Sometimes, we allow what happened yesterday to determine our future. We live in a world where we walk with shame and struggle to be free. Don't let the shame of your past make you believe you don't have the power within to step into what you want to be. Don't let the past failures make you think you can't bounce back for greatness. Your past wasn't meant to kill you, but it was established to build you. The past is in the past, so don't let anyone hold you to your past mistakes. When folks try to remind you of your past, tell them how you made it over, and how you made it through. God places our eyes in the front and not in the back.

We have to learn how to forgive so we can walk free and to blossom into what God created us to be. When we are dealing with unforgiveness, we are putting ourselves in a stronghold that is killing us, and that can hinder us from walking into the next level of life. As a speaker and an educator, I always hear folks say, *"If you just understood my past, you would understand why I walk in shame. If you just understood my past, you would understand why I am a failure and why I can't move forward because of it."* Understand, it's not about what you go through, but it's about how you respond to what you go through. I tell folks, just because I haven't been in theirs shoes, it doesn't mean I don't have a struggle of my own.

Shame was not a part of God's identity or creation when He put us in this world. Guilt is a part of the enemy's techniques, and he uses it, so you won't get what God has in store for you. The enemy will make you feel so ashamed of yourself, where you feel like you don't matter, aren't valued, and can't be validated. The beginning does not determine the final results of your life. We have to be willing to accept failure because it is not always bad. How can we succeed if we don't fail? Sometimes, we have to fail to bounce back. You won't know what success feels like if we never been through the process of failing. For growth to take place in life, we have to accept failure, and accepting defeat does not mean that you are a failure, but it's making you recognize that there are some things that demand growth from you. To become the goal setters and goal hitters, we have to let go of shame from the past. Don't be ashamed if you're failing; everyone goes through hardships. When you do bounce back, you will bounce back much stronger, wiser, and better. The only way you can't bounce back from the setbacks of life is when your mindset is a mindset of failure and not a success. Choose to embrace the hardships because the hardships will turn into a great purpose in the end.

What are you ashamed about? Do you choose to stay in shame from your past failures? If so, ask yourself why? So many of us are finding ourselves repeating cycles, and we are wondering why we can't move forward. When we choose to stay in shame, we are also choosing not to grow.

The acronym that I wrote for shame is:

Self

Hate

After

Making

Errors

Shame that stems from trauma causes us not to want to talk about the pain. It bothers you so much that there are times when you may have nightmares of that situation or scenario happening again. You may be afraid of what people will think if you reveal your trauma. The beginning of the healing process is sharing your story. When you share your story, you will be able to release the pain on the inside. We can't hold on to things that happened years ago because it's out of our control. We can't change the past, but we do have control over our future. When you keep thinking about your past, your life will soon become a repeat of your past. Life demands growth from you, and it's impossible to grow when you are stuck in yesterday.

There's a story about a young woman named Taylor. Taylor was a woman who seemed like everything was going right for her. She stayed smiling, pursuing hard, running hard, and she was also the person people would go to for advice about life situations. She could tell you things to do, and you would see it flourish right in front of your eyes. She gave excellent advice, and people started calling her their life counselor. If anything was going wrong, they would reach out to Taylor because she had the right words for the moment. At some point in time, she met a fella by the name of Roger. Roger came to Taylor and talked to her about everything that he was going through, even his deep secrets that nobody else knew. While he was sharing his story, Taylor started crying. One thing that Roger didn't know was the reason why she was crying, and he thought to himself that maybe he said something wrong that offended her, or perhaps she was feeling empathy for him. Minutes pass, and Taylor wept tears. However, she didn't know what to tell Roger. He was sharing the very thing she had shame about for years.

Eventually, Taylor got herself together, and after fourteen years of this shame, she was dealing with what Roger was talking about. Taylor had deep wounds that nobody knew about because she was good at faking a smile and making it look real. She had scars since she was a baby, but nobody knew about them because she never showed her pain. She paused and told Roger, "I know what you are going through." Taylor showed Roger the cuts on her arm; she had been cutting herself since she was ten years old.

She believed that cutting herself was the best way to ease the pain that was going on inside of her. She shared that she didn't feel like she was accepted by other people because of the shame of what happened 14 years ago. When she was done sharing, Roger shared his story with Taylor. One of the things they both had in common was that their wounds lasted more than 12 years were never talked about. Roger showed Taylor his cuts. He felt relief. When the conversation was over, the first thing they both said was: "Wow, that feels good. Now I feel like I can walk with my head high. I never knew that people even understood what I could be going through. I am just happy that I met someone who has been in the same mess that I was in. Thank you for listening and not judging while I share."

Just because we see folks smile, doesn't mean they are happy. You know you can feel lonely even when you are in the midst of company. In this story, we see a woman who gave good advice, and the information she was offering was right on point. She gave the advice to help others, but she was broken and wounded herself. She was good at holding up a great outward appearance. When Taylor was hurt, it didn't stop her from advising others. The great news from this story is that she was able to walk free from bondage because of the hope she received from Roger.

I want you to know that there's still hope. You do not know who needs to hear your story so they can get a breakthrough. Don't let what happened yesterday be the voice of your today and tomorrow. Don't let what happened years ago become your excuse not to be great. Talk about the hurts with people who won't judge you.

I remember when I was hurting, wounded, and bruised because of past hurts that I never dealt with; I was hurting other people, because hurting people hurt people. I didn't recognize that what I was doing was hurting people. It wasn't until I got wrapped in the arms of my mentor, who took me in as his own, and loved me despite of me, that I started to walk into freedom. Don't let the pain of your past build up for so long that you don't recognize the folks you're hurting are just trying to love you. I didn't realize the folks who were reaching out to me in the midst of my pain were trying to build me and help me because I was blinded by pain.

Love is a treatment, and hate is a curse.

I remember going back to the folks who I had hurt to apologize to them because I didn't realize the damage that I'd caused. They didn't know what I was going through, but they knew something was going on; through it all, they still chose to love me because they knew that love is what cures pain. To become goal setters and goal hitters, we have to be able to forgive ourselves so we can have the power to forgive others. Genuine forgiveness can't happen if we do not deal with self-hurt. It starts with us before it can start flowing out in the community.

6. Choosing To Do Nothing

For many of us, we have decided to do nothing, and that decision is hurting us. A wasted life is also a wasted future, and a wasted future is also a wasted legacy, and a wasted legacy turns into a curse instead of a blessing. What are you doing to make sure your dreams become reality? When you have a mentality of nothingness, you will have a lifestyle of being content. We were not born to be ordinary; we were born to do extraordinary things.

The trials and tribulations in life are like boot camp. In the first several weeks of boot camp, you are going to be tired, frustrated, and you might want to give up. In the process of working out, you are going to be sore, and you will be going through some pain until your body gets adjusted to the workout. That's the same as the trials and tribulations that we go through. We may want to throw in the towel, but don't! You will never know how much you have within you until you get to the point of being broken. In the midst of the brokenness, you have two choices — bounce back or live defeated.

Goal hitters and goal setters, understand that choosing to do nothing should never be an option or even a thought. Goal setters who are goal hitters know that the moment they decide to do nothing is the moment they waste a minute of impact and influence. Until you unleash the person on the inside that wants to win, you will only make excuses. Let the winner on the inside lose to win! I want you to understand that greatness doesn't happen outside, it all happens inside of you. Your full potential comes from the inside. Choosing to do nothing comes from a defeated mentality. Until you decide to respond to your situations differently, you will never be able to release what is within.

7. Believe

Believing is the foundation for achieving our dreams. Often, we get our dreams crushed, and that makes it hard for us to believe again. Having a vision for your goals is not seeing it first; it's believing. The foundation of life is belief.

The belief you have in yourself determines your mindset. What do you believe about yourself? What caused you to think this way? Some of us find that what we believe about ourselves comes from messages the media and past life experiences. Believing is the foundation of greatness, and if we are not careful, we can hinder our greatness because of the lack of faith. We reap what we sow, and if we are not careful with what we are sowing into our life, then we can reap adverse outcomes. Speak what you want into the atmosphere, they are prophesying our tomorrow.

You can never step into the best version of yourself until you unleash the real you that is on the inside. The you that you are afraid to show others around you. The you that craves success more than anything. The you that is telling you to give the best you with no limitations and no regrets. There is a part of you that wants what is best for you!

People who are goal setters and goal hitters understand that believing is the key to winning. Muhammad Ali once said, *"Champions aren't made in gyms. Champions are made from something they have deep inside them, a desire, a dream, a vision. They have to have last-minute stamina, they have to be a little faster, they have to have skill and the will. But the will must be stronger than the skill."* When you lack self-belief, you will tend to believe anything that is coming your way. When you don't have a firm foundation in life, you will be like a house that is trying to be built without a solid foundation. Understand the foundation of life is to believe. Believe even if nobody else believes in you. Believe even if nobody else stands with you. Believe even if nobody else can see you achieving what you desire. At the end of the day, it doesn't matter about the other voices. The voice that matters most is your voice. When a negative thought comes, you have to be able to speak positivity.

Your "why" in life must be greater than your doubt. Without going through trials and tribulations, we will never be able to see what we really believe about ourselves. You define where life takes you based on what you think about you. So, it's time to change your stinking thinking. Don't give up even if you feel defeated. You can overcome what may look like is hard to beat if you just believe that you can. You can become great no matter what the circumstance might be in your life as long as you just believe that there's greatness from within. When you make believing the foundation of your life, nothing in this world can stop you from doing what you want to do. Sometimes we don't think that we have enough strength within to push through, so we tend to stay comfortable because we don't want to feel or be uncomfortable.

8. Blocking the Voices of Negativity

The more negativity you block, the more you will find yourself stepping into bigger and better things. The first step starts with you. Be careful when listening to particular radio stations. Pay attention to the words that you are speaking to yourself. If these words are negative, you are affirming negativity in your life. If you don't rebuke a negative thought, you are giving those thoughts access to come back. And once they do come back, eventually you're going to think they are the truth for your life. What messages are you rehearsing that are holding you back from becoming the best you? What are you tuning into? You have to be careful with what you say to yourself and what you are downloading into your life.

I remember seeing this VISION in the 8th grade, and it gave me hope and so much motivation to keep on going. When folks were speaking negatively about me, I saw an opportunity to keep on going on. The words they were speaking were like a refueling, giving me gas to keep on thriving. Years go by, and I keep speaking positive words into existence. I didn't give up. In 9th grade, nothing happens, 10th grade nothing happens, and 11th grade nothing happens. Then BOOM, I'm stepping into the 12th grade, and I got involved in this after-school program called Peer Health Council. It was run by an organization named "CSC" (Community Schools & Collaboration). This program catered to students who felt like they were leaders and wanted to impact their school and city. I signed up for this, and I said yes, that is me. I am a leader in multiple ways, and I want to change things that I see affecting my community, my city, and my school. I gave my all to this after-school program. I made sure this was a priority in my life.

The site director, Karly Feria comes to me and says, *"We have an opportunity for someone to speak at a national conference in Kansas City, Missouri. We can't take everybody; we can only take one person. If you want to go, you have to submit a reason why you want to go and why you believe you will be a good candidate for this and why your message is important at this conference. Also, you need to have at least three letters of recommendation from people in your school."*

I was on it. This program was held in four schools and one person was selected from each school. I wrote my letter and I received the recommendations back in three days after I asked for them. Once I got everything, I gave it to the Site Director and it had to go to a board for them to read it and go over it, to make a decision. Within two weeks after submission, I got a notice that I was selected to speak at the ASHA (American School Health Association) national conference where there would be teachers, lawyers, educational board members, doctors and many other important people. I would speak about the lack of training teachers have when working with kids with disabilities and discrimination. I remember this moment as if it just happened yesterday. I remember coming home and telling my family that I am going to speak at a National conference. I was so excited about this opportunity; I couldn't help but say, 'Wow, my first speaking gig is at age seventeen.'

My first platform of speaking was at a conference where I was speaking to five hundred plus people in Kansas City, MO. I felt connected to the audience; I saw tears in some of the attendees' eyes as I told my story. Once I was on that stage, I felt like I was born to be on the mic, a change-maker, and a voice for the voiceless. I knew this was my purpose. I remember coming back to Seattle and the lead, Amanda, shared with us that we got rated for our speaking, and she wanted to share what the audience thought about our presentations. In my head, I said, "I hope it won't be too harsh because I am just 17."

I believed I did alright but I knew I could have done better. I remember receiving the papers and looking at the feedback, and I couldn't help but cry; I was astonished by the results! My rating was good. On the back of the scores were notes, and the notes I received blew me away. I asked myself if this was even real. After that, I was invited to come and speak at other conferences in different locations.

When I got back to school, my peers were wondering how I got picked because they didn't believe in me. The city of Sea-Tac invited me to come and speak for their 20th anniversary. When I was done speaking, different individuals encouraged me not to give up.

While transitioning from high school to college, I started claiming what I wanted in life; I told myself that this would be the season where I will be traveling and speaking in schools, communities, conferences, and much more.

During my first two years in college, I was at Highline Community College, located in Des-Moines, WA. I landed a position as a work-study student as a Student Ambassador, which is a part of the outreach department on campus. The role of the ambassador was to give tours to prospective students who were inquiring about the school. I also went to different schools and shared my story. I landed my dream job, and it prepared me for more speaking engagements. After working in that position for two years and blocking the voices of negativity, I had schools, businesses, organizations, and churches call me to see if they could book me to speak at different events. I am sharing this story to say that there will be people in your life who are not going to believe what you believe about yourself. If you just believe, you can achieve whatever you want. If I listened to the words of other people, I would have never had the opportunity to travel and speak out of state at a young age. Your dreams are your dreams, and if you don't have a plan to get there, then those dreams are just wishes. Hang in there and fight!

Martin Luther Kind once said, *"Faith is taking the first step even when you don't see the whole staircase. "*You were not meant to see everything before you believe it. You were meant to take the first step and see everything else manifest. If you believe in your "why," would you fight even if it means taking your last breath? Your "why'" becomes your drive, and when your why becomes your drive, then your drive will be your results.

9. Circle of Influence

A wise man once told me, *"What you do in your life will determine what you leave behind and what you plant in your life will determine how far you go in your life."* Our circle of influence plays a significant role in our life. Sometimes, we can't manifest the best because we have people in our circle who are poisoning our outlook. Some of us are attached to people that we should never be connected too. We have soul ties that should be broken, and we attract people just like us. Are you willing to cut people out of your life so you can step into the best part of life? Your circle is just a reflection of who you are. If your circle is not building you, then it's killing you. If your circle is not pushing you where it's uncomfortable, then you are in the wrong circle of people. They should push you and hold you accountable for your actions.

43

I remember growing up, I always told myself what I wanted to be, but there were some issues that I had never dealt with. It wasn't until I attacked those issues that I started seeing my dreams become a reality. When our foundation is broken, and we don't attack the problems when they are small, they will start growing, and eventually, what happens is we attract other broken people into our lives. When you have a broken foundation, a broken mindset, a broken circle, you will reap brokenness, shame, guilt, pain, and wounds that have nothing to do with others. Our sphere of influence should be healthy.

You can't say that you're a visionary, and then, surround yourself with folks who are visionless. You can't have everybody in your circle because not everybody deserves to be in your circle. You have to protect the energy coming into your life because if you don't, you will have to reap a negative outcome. Whatever type of people you draw into your circle, you will start manifesting how they manifest because of the seeds they plant. You should cherish and protect your life, your goals, your dreams, and visions with all your heart and powers. If not, you will find yourself walking towards a path of destruction because of what you are bringing into your life. Your circle can be an asset or a liability you choose.

Change Your Mindset, and You Will Change Who You Are

Do you know the reason why we always see a crow everywhere, but it's rare to see an Eagle? When we compare goal setters and visionaries, we have to understand that the crow is a goal maker, and the eagle is a visionary. These are two birds, but these birds have different traits and characteristics. An eagle has excellent vision; it can focus on something up to fifty kilometers away; the eagle will never surrender to the size or strength of its prey; it will always fight to win and regain its territory. In Isaiah 40:30-31 it says: *"Even the youths shall faint and be weary, and the young men shall utterly fall: But they who wait upon the Lord shall renew their strength; they shall mount up with wings as eagles; they shall run, and not be weary; they shall walk, and not faint."*

The Lord wants us to be like eagles and focus on our destination. Crows and Eagles don't hang together. Pick your friends carefully. We have to have a vision and remain so focused that no matter what the trial might be, if we stay focused, then we shall succeed. The question we have to answer is: 'Who are the crows in our life?' Every step you take should be taken with a purpose. There are people in our lives that are hindering us, and we have a choice to either cut them out of our lives or keep them in our lives. Some people don't understand that friendships should be earned and not just given. When I say that this person is my friend, I am also saying that they have a right to keep me accountable because we have built a relationship that we can hold each other accountable. If you can't see your friends holding you accountable, then why do you have them as your friend? My mentor once told me, "*If you are the smartest one in your circle, then you are in the wrong circle.*" I asked my mentor why, then he responded, "Because there should be someone smarter than you." Let that sink in for a minute! (re-read that quote) Release folks in your life that are not bearing the good fruits that you may want to witness out of your life.

CHAPTER THREE

ENDURING STRUGGLES
THAT LEAD TO GREATNESS

Hello everybody, welcome to the life simulation event where we will be discussing how to endure the struggle that leads to greatness. By a show of hands, how many people believe that every battle a person endures leads to greatness? (only a few hands go up) If you don't believe it, why? If you do believe it, why? Many of them did not believe greatness could come from pain.

There's a motto that says, *"Go Big or Go Home."* It means to give your all in whatever you are doing and if you're not willing to give your all in whatever you are doing, then don't start. Going big means doing what makes you uncomfortable. Going big means going beyond even though it hurts. Many want to see the big things manifest in their lives, but not many are willing to start with the small things that lead to big things. You can't build a house without beginning with the foundation.

Some may ask, how can greatness come out of this situation? One thing that we have to understand about the struggles is, you must build yourself and push yourself towards your purpose. The struggles you endure are only temporary and it may feel like they are permanent. Without a mess, there can't be a message, and without a test, there can't be a testimony. I believe that everybody has had to endure a hardship that has pushed them towards their purpose.

In Romans chapter 5:1-4 (NIV Version) it says, *"Therefore, since we have been justified through faith, we have peace with God through our Lord Jesus Christ, through him we have gained access by faith into this grace in which we now stand. And we boast in the hope of the glory of God. Not only so, but we also glory in our sufferings, because we know that suffering produces perseverance; perseverance produces character; and character produces hope."*

When I read the last passage that says suffering produces perseverance, I feel relieved. Suffering produces perseverance and perseverance produces character and character produces hope. We first have to make sure that our response to our sufferings and struggles is an overcomer response. People have this belief that if they do not go through anything, then it will be much easier to get what they want in life. I truly believe that if people don't go through anything, then it will be much harder for them. Let me explain. If you don't go through any test, then you don't have a testimony and if you don't encounter any mess, then you won't have a message. If you don't face any roadblocks in life, then you can't develop your character. Suffering is what produces perseverance and perseverance produces character.

There are some icons we can use as an example in life. Let's talk about one who stepped into the NBA, and made a name for himself, LeBron James. LeBron is one of the best players in the league and some say that he is the best of all time. We see him as this basketball player who is great at what he does but what we don't see is the sacrifices that he made to get to where he is at today. He didn't become great immediately but there were some things he had to do in order for greatness to be manifested.

According to an article on NBA.com, "*My Amazing Journey – LeBron James,*" LeBron talked about the obstacles that he had to encounter before he got to the NBA. When asked what the biggest obstacle he overcame to reach the NBA was, he said, "*Just going through some of the struggles I went through as a kid and not taking it personal, and just hopping over obstacles and going through speed bumps. It was not always a bad road for me as a kid, and I understood that. But, at the same time, it was tough. So, I think the trials and tribulations I went through as a kid really helped me get to this point.*"

The first thing we notice about LeBron is that he understands his struggle is what pushed him to where he is. He embraced the hardships he endured as a child. If we welcome difficulties, they can lead us to greatness. Today, we see LeBron's legacy in the NBA. What legacy do you want to carry? Life is not about how you start; it's all about how you finish. We can't control what happens in life, but we can control how we respond to what happens in life. Life will knock you down, but you have the option to either stay down or get back up. Sometimes, we let how we begin, dictate how we finish.

Let's think of the Seattle Seahawks. The Hawks played many games, and the first half made it seem as if they would lose. However, they didn't give up. There have been games when Seattle came back the 2nd half and won the game. The team didn't let how the game began to determine how they were going to end. If we just fight the good fight, then we will win this. The team didn't let the scoreboard determine the outcome.

Don't let the struggle that you are going through become the voice for your final destination. Suffering has a purpose. Nothing you go through can triumph over you unless you give it the power to triumph over you. Your "why" can't be manifested if you don't go through anything in life.

I remember being a senior in high school, and I attended SCORE (Students of Color Opting to Reach Excellence) conference at the Highline College. In the 2nd half of this conference, they opened the mic up for students to share their gifts and talents. While networking and meeting new people, I went and mingled with my peers, and I remember talking to this lady who is now my good friend, Niela Hampton, who is the Co-Director for a non-profit called Freshest Roots in Seattle, WA. I mentioned that I'm a poet, and she said she was also. Her eyes got all big, and she said, "Oh, you should perform." I responded and said, "Oh no, I won't do that." We went back and forth, and finally, we both got up to perform and inspire the students.

Another young lady went and grabbed the mic. She looked at me and said, "*I remember you. You changed my life last year with your story. I want to let you know, for the past three years, I have been going through challenges, and I didn't know how to handle it. I heard your story, and you shared your poetry piece, and that changed my life completely.*" She went on and said, "*I was going to drop out because I didn't see the value or the purpose anymore. I wanted to throw in the towel, but because of you, I am now finishing high school and now pushing for my best life. I want to say thank you.*" I hugged her, and she hugged me back. That was a good day! It might be tough talking about your tribulations and pain, but if it helps another person, then it's worth it. Everyone in life goes through hardships, but not everyone in life uses those hardships as an opportunity for impact. Below are examples of how enduring struggles can lead to greatness.

1. Seeing Your Reflection:

Mahatma Gandhi once said, "Be the change you wish to see in the world." Before a change in the world can take place, we have to change ourselves. We can't change a community if we can't change who we are as individuals. A changed man can bring a community change, and a broken man can break a community. The question is, which one are you? Are you willing to do what it takes to be the change? Will you sit down and complain about issues? This is a question that we have to ask ourselves. When we don't deal with the reflection in the mirror, it becomes a struggle that seems like it will never end.

I remember doing AmeriCorps through Washington Service Corps and working as a Program Coordinator at Madrona Elementary, located in Sea-Tac, WA. In this after school program, I had kids from 3rd - 6th grade yearning to learn and grow. As a Program Coordinator, my role was to create plans for these kids. Over time, the kids started trusting me; they started being real with me and talking about things they dealt with but had no idea how to resolve it. I found out that most of the children were dealing with issues children shouldn't have to bear.

I began to pull each kid to the side throughout the weeks, to talk about many different things. One thing I always asked the kids is this, "When you see yourself in the mirror, what do you tell yourself? What about your reflection, do you like, and what don't you like?" One thing I realize is, it was easier for the kids to talk about what they did not like about themselves than it was for them to talk about what they did like about themselves.

While working with the kids I've come to the conclusion that 63% of the kids said greatness couldn't come out of their struggles, and 37% said that greatness would come out of what they were going through. When talking with adults, one of the questions that were asked was, *"Who believes there is power in self-reflection?"* Not many raised hands. Then the second question I asked was, *"Do you see more positive or negative when you ponder your life?"* When I talked to the adults, 55% of them said they couldn't tap into greatness because of what they had gone through or what they were currently going through, and 45% said they believed they could tap into greatness and what they were going through would push them into greatness. By comparing kids and adults, I realized that there's a problem with how individuals view themselves. A positive identity must be fostered as a child so that we can achieve greatness.

Martin Luther King once said, *"The ultimate measure of a man is not where he stands in moments of comfort and convenience, but where he stands at times of challenge and controversy."*

The trials and tribulations happen in life so you can see your own reflection. You will never know what you believe about yourself until you go through hardships. It's easy to act confident, but are you convinced that a break-through will come when life is getting out of hand. It's easy to talk the talk, but can you walk the walk?

You will never tap into your "why" if you don't tap into self-reflection. Michael Jackson once said, *"If you want to make the world a better place, you got to look at yourself and make that change."* A lot of us have aspirations, dreams, and goals but tend to give up when the fork hits the road.

The trials and tribulations of life have to happen to step into the next chapters of life. Greatness is a process, and without enduring the struggles, greatness can't manifest. We have to embrace the setbacks in life because it's the setbacks that will cause a major bounce back. Doors that you never thought would be open will open. Opportunities will arrive when self-reflection happens. This process of self-evaluation is a time for development and growth.

2. It's Part Of The Process

A professor is always quiet in the middle of a test. The professor can't answer questions that you may have because the test will determine what you have learned throughout the course. It will reveal what you understand and what you don't understand. However, if you don't pass the test, you might have to take the class all over again.

Before you can go to the next level, you have to understand your current level. Throughout life, you have been planting seeds in your life that declare things in the atmosphere, and what you say attracts things and people in your life. What you go through is the beginning process of stepping into the best version of you. If you can't embrace the setbacks, it will be hard for you to step into the bounce backs.

I remember going through the storms and the heartaches, and for a long time, I was contemplating committing suicide. Life was getting out of hand, and I couldn't control it any longer. I started planning how I wanted to end my life because I felt like I was not valued. I didn't think anybody cared about me or my wellbeing. I was planning my death because I felt like life was too hard. Even though I knew I would never have the guts to do anything to end my life, I still felt like I didn't have the strength to keep living.

I grew up in church and went through the motions; I was a part of VBS (Vacation Bible School), my dad was a Pastor/Bishop over several Haitian churches back home in Haiti. I went through the motions of church and smiled my way through, but nobody knew what was going on. My family and the church people didn't know what was going on. It wasn't that I was afraid to share it, I didn't know how to share it.

Throughout life, I masked my pain; for me, this was just the way of life. I eventually attempted to commit suicide, which I failed miserably. I ran across the street, in the middle of incoming traffic, and I made it to the other side while traffic was coming. Then, I ran across the other side during the incoming traffic, and I made it to the other side. I was a junior in high school at the time, and I suddenly remembered a scripture that my VBS teacher told me when I was a young kid. The scripture was 1 Corinthians10:13 (NIV), which reads, *"No temptation has overtaken you except what is common to mankind. And God is faithful; he will not let you be tempted beyond what you can bear. But when you are tempted, he will also provide a way out so that you can endure it."* That scripture came to me after I made it to the other side, and at that moment, an overwhelming peace came over me. I felt freedom, and I believed that there was a purpose for me in this world.

The following day, I had folks ask me if I was okay, what was going on, and that they were concerned with my wellbeing after hearing that I'd attempted to commit suicide. I recall an overflow of letters in my locker from people telling me they loved me, how I inspired them and motivated them and that they are here for me anytime. I remember people coming to me after school crying and hugging me and telling me that if I ever needed a place to stay, their homes would always be available. I know what if feels like to have suicidal thoughts and feel like you're not valued or loved.

My response to what I was going through was the way it was because I have downloaded some things in my life that were not part of God's identity for me. I have planted some seeds in my life that turned into a stronghold that became hard to break. However, I am free today; I no longer have suicidal thoughts. I am free because I left my problems in God's hands. God cleaned me from the inside out. Now, I walk with integrity with a real genuine smile on my face, and I have a pure love for others.

Months later, after this event took place in my life, I got asked to come to speak to these kids who wanted to give up on life. The person who asked me to come and speak to these kids had no idea that I'd attempted suicide myself. I remember it as if this was yesterday. I walked into a room with twenty-five kids who were 10th -12th graders who had known and hidden disabilities. I was in a panel with eleven other people of color who had disabilities that were sharing their story with these kids.

In the audience, there were kids and their parents. While I was sharing my story, I started seeing the kids wiping their tears. My story hit them in a way that they weren't expecting to be hit. I didn't only talk about the darkness, but I spoke of the light, hope, and the assurance of purpose. I talked about how God saved me in May 2010 on 188th street by Tyee High School, located in SeaTac, WA.

Once I was done sharing my story, it was time for Q&As from the audience. While the questions were rising from the kids and their families, I let them know that the best way to release what needs to be released from within is by letting it out.

"If that means you have to cry, then please go ahead and cry. Don't apologize for the tears you are shedding because this is the beginning of a healing process." At that moment, I knew that I had to encounter what I encountered, to be able to shine a light and bring hope to

someone else who needs to hear how to overcome suffering, heartaches, trials, and tribulations.

You will never be able to bring hope to someone else if you don't have a story that brings transformation to someone else. Through your story, hope, strength, and healing rise. Through your story, breakthroughs take place, and victory occurs. No one can tell your story better than you.

If you are not willing to trust the process, then you are not ready to grow and step into your full potential. A lot of us want growth but are not willing to go through the process to receive an increase. How serious are you about wanting to see things shift in your life? How determined are you to see good manifest?

If you say you are serious and determined, then leave the excuses behind and embrace the process. The process might be tough, and it might hurt, and that's okay. You are being stretched to a level that you have never experienced. The level is to build, equip, shape, and mold you for greatness.

3. LEGACY

We live in a time that some people don't think about their legacy. How do you want people to remember you? What do you want folks to say about you? Do you want folks to remember you as the individual who tends to quit when times get rough? Or do you want people to remember you as the individual who fought a good fight?

Generational curses happen; we don't change the broken behaviors of our past. But you have the power to turn things around in your life, and to pass it down to your family. Just because you grew up in a hostile environment does not mean that you have to create that environment for your family. Are you even thinking about the legacy, and what is being left behind? Or are you just living life for the now? Behind every legacy, there's a story that comes with it. Don't look at what you went through with a broken lens but look at it through a legacy lens. Your family will watch you and copy that same pattern of behavior.

Legacy says there's a fight in this life, and I want to give my kids everything. I refuse to settle for less and repeat the circumstances that I had to encounter. Legacy says, I know how that pain feels, and I refuse to pass that pain down to generations after me. Some of us want to leave blessings but don't want to encounter the storms of life that can turn into blessings. Your legacy is not defined by what you are going through, but how you respond to what you are going through.

As an educator, speaker, and trainer around youth development and professional development, I always ask the audience why they chose the field that they wanted. What inspired them to step into their field? The career that we are in can impact or destroy lives. I remember asking educators who teach K-12 why they teach. About 45% of the educators stated that they are in the field because they went to school for this, and 30% said they like kids and always wanted to work with kids. Another 25% of educators said they love kids and want to inspire them to become better. We need teachers who are teaching because they want to be there, not because it's a job. Immediately, I find myself talking directly with the people who were just doing it because it was a job, and I asked them if they understand legacy.

I remember, in 2012, I was part of an educational panel called WABSE (Washington Association Board for Students Education) with Erin Jones, who was a candidate running for the Washington State Superintendent of Public Instruction against Chris Reykdal. This was an opportunity for educators and people who have thought about going into education to ask college students of color questions regarding our experiences in the K-12 system. I remember the audience being white, while the panel, who were folks of color and from different backgrounds of life. I remember sitting on the panel and telling people around me that there was a problem, that we had to reach the audience, and the problem was the lack of representation that our schools have. For a lot of people, and especially educators, their focus is not legacy. While being on the panel, I didn't see any diversity, and that was a problem.

I asked the question, *"What is the best way to connect with students of color?"* I remember looking at my mentor, and he's looking at me, and I am looking at my best friend, and he's looking at me. I took a minute and paused to figure out what is the best way to answer this question. I let the audience know, the best way to connect to children of color is first connecting to your purpose. The love you have for them will determine if you connect or not. This is not just for students of color; this is for every student. I believe all educators need diversity and equity training. As an educator, you have a footprint you are leaving in the hallways of the schools.

When the event was over, a lady came and asked me, "What do you think should be the role of a teacher who has kids for eight hours a day or more?" I let this teacher know that the position should consist of positive leadership for all ethnicities. I let her know that everybody needs to think about legacy and then lead from that place.

What is your footprint? Everybody is watching you, and they will follow your lead. It's about "reach one; teach one." I am reaching out to you to help you, help others. Someone did this for me years ago. This individual reached out and gave back to his community in a way that impacted my life. My life is forever changed because of him. This individual wasn't just talking the talk, but he was walking the walk. He left a legacy for his family and the community. This man is still my mentor, father figure, friend, and a coach to me in multiple ways. His name is Rashad Norris.

Mr. Norris had uplifting energy and a spirit that brought hope in a room. I remember hearing that an African American man would be coming to campus to speak to the youth, and I was asked by a teacher to come down to listen to this man speak. Something about him grabbed my attention; I believe it was because this man looked like me. I sat right in front of the class while he was talking. He had so much love for the people that you could sense it. I sat there as he dropped knowledge, and I soaked it all up. After he was done, he gave me his business card, and told me that he wanted to mentor me and be there for me. He looked directly into my eyes and said to me that he loved me and that he wanted to help me grow.

Within the next following weeks, I called him, and we connected, and we have stayed in touch ever since. Every time I called Mr. Norris, he was there and followed through, he made time to come see me and check up on me. He treated me like his son. The legacy that he left in my life taught me that I could fight and overcome anything. Before you throw in the towel, ask yourself this question, *"What is the legacy that I want to leave?"*

Michael Jackson sang a song that goes like this, *"I'm starting with the man in the mirror. I'm asking him to change his ways. And no message could have been any clearer, if you wanna make the world a better place take a look at yourself and then make a change."* Change is necessary.

One of the biggest life lessons that my father passed down to his kids, is the legacy of prayer. As a young child, my dad taught us the word of God, and that was our foundation. My father would be up late at night praying for hours, and even when his kids were sleeping, he would bless the whole house with prayer. My dad taught me how to pray even in difficult times. You couldn't tell my dad that something was impossible because he would make sure it became possible.

I witnessed my dad praying on his knees in both difficult and good times. He put his full trust in God. My dad was the man who would pray with you, pray for you, and fight whatever you were fighting. My family's foundation was prayer. I am grateful that my dad had faith in God.

On October 27th, 2018, I found myself calling out to God with tears in my eyes. It was a war cry for help that I learned from my father. I was on E Marginal way in Seattle, heading home. All of a sudden, I start having chest issues; my heart was pounding so hard that it was affecting my driving. My head was down on the steering wheel, and when I looked up, I found myself on the other side of the road facing incoming traffic, lights were beaming in my face. The lights were so bright I couldn't keep my eyes open. I closed my eyes and called on the name of Jesus. I said, "God, you have to take the wheel. I cannot die like this; this can't be the day that I am going to die." All of a sudden, I open my eyes to find myself on the other side of the road. Now, I am on Pacific Highway off of 216th St. in Des-Moines, WA, and all of a sudden, my legs start shaking. I have shaky legs and a pounding chest, I am crying, and saying, *"Josias is going to live, he is not going to die."* I started to pray out loud, *"God, I am proclaiming your healing and breakthrough. I rebuke the plans of the enemy and what he is trying to do. God, I don't know what this is about, but I am proclaiming victory right now over my body."*

Then, and all of a sudden, my fingers start tingling. I knew at that moment I had to pull over and call 911. When I called, the dispatcher could barely understand what I was saying because my voice was weak. I was mumbling my words, I could barely talk, my fingers were tingly, my legs shaking, my chest pounding, and my mouth and tongue were swollen. The dispatcher said they would get someone to me. Finally, the paramedics showed up, 60 minutes after I'd called. I let the dispatchers know that the paramedics arrived, and we got off the phone. The medics approached me and started to ask me questions, and I let them know I didn't have time to answer questions; I needed to go to the hospital. They were taking their sweet time. It didn't seem like I was getting the care I deserved.

At the hospital the doctors tried to run a test to check my blood pressure, and they didn't get anything! I was crying, and I told the doctors that I must be dying. They also did an ultrasound and couldn't find anything. Now, I am panicking and calling on the name of Jesus. From the moment the pain started until it stopped, I was calling on Jesus. I felt like I was having a stroke, but the doctors refused to acknowledge this.

The doctors eventually did an EKG to check if there was anything out of the ordinary; they came back and informed me that my heart was fine. It was determined that I was okay and that I was having an anxiety attack. I let the doctors know that if they didn't find anything wrong, then it was an attack of the enemy. I let the doctors know that I believed this was a spiritual attack. I told them that I believe that God healed me, and they were amazed.

This experience was a humbling experience for me because it showed me how much faith I have in God. I am grateful that my dad taught us how to pray and read our word so we would know how to fight the enemy.

4. Hunger

The hunger I am referring to is not food or starvation. One of my mentors is Les Brown, and one thing that Les Brown always says is, *"You got to be hungry!"* I remember sitting in the Comcast Arena, waiting to hear him speak. Les Brown faced many adversities in his life, but he never quit. I remember hearing his life story and shedding tears with my business partner because I could relate to him so much. When he said you got to be hungry, everything in me could relate! Mr. Brown once said, *"If you take responsibility for yourself, you will develop a hunger to accomplish your dreams."* So many of us make excuses, and we miss the opportunity to make our circumstances better because of these reasons.

Being a kid with special needs, I had many people in my life who didn't see that I could become better than my limitations. A lot of people made assumptions because of my disability. However, I was hungry for more! I was so hungry to make my dreams a reality, and I knew there was a purpose for what I was going through. I was willing to do what many thought was impossible. Because of my hunger, my dreams have become a reality. I have spoken in many conferences where I was the keynote speaker and facilitated workshops to empower people.

The hunger that you have for greatness will become your drive for life. Greatness determines a craving, and when you have a craving, then you will be hungry for it, and when you are hungry for it, you will do anything to make it possible. What are you doing right now to make your dreams become a reality? Are you taking action? Or are you making excuses? There are 24 hours in a day; how many hours are you using to ensure your vision comes to life? A wise man once said, *"How you train will show when it's time for war."* Are you prepared? The question is, what voice will you believe? Will you believe the voice that says you can't do it? Or will you believe the voice that says, you can do it? When life gets hard, and it seems like everything is falling apart, don't quit.

CHAPTER FOUR

STAND UP FOR WHAT'S RIGHT

Throughout history, many movements such as Civil Rights, Women's Rights, and Labor Right's took place to bring change in communities. If we fast forward to 2013, people organized a movement called "Black Lives Matter". The awareness it brought was justice and equality for black people. Some people say, *"I don't believe black lives matter, I believe all lives matter."* When people say this sentence, I don't think they understand what they are saying. You can't say you believe all lives matter but don't believe that black lives matter. What is black life? This movement was founded on July 13, 2013 by three beautiful black women whose names are, Alicia Garza, Patrisse Cullors, & Opal Tometi. The designed purpose of the movement was to shine a light on issues that have plagued America; however, most white America refuses to acknowledge them.

This movement brought communities together from all across the world to fight for a purpose. This is a movement that is needed and will always be needed because America needs to understand that black and brown life is just as important and valuable as white lives. When people are saying, "Black Lives Matter" they are not saying only black lives matter, they are saying, the world is treating black and brown people like their lives are not valued. Many times, when we hear "Black Lives Matter" we automatically think of police brutality. However, it goes deeper than police brutality. If we look into any system that was built in America, we will see that the system never benefited people of color to begin with.

What makes taking a knee offensive? Some say it's disrespecting the flag and those who fought for our country. If we look deeper into the history of the flag, we will see how it does not represent people of color. There are verses in the anthem that we don't sing because they don't uplift people of color.

The pledge of allegiance talks about liberty, justice for all, but they are not present for all Americans. Tim Tebow took a knee to pray; everyone was silent. People have said if anyone takes a knee during the national anthem, they can't respect that individual because they are disrespectful. Yet, Tim Tebow took a knee, and nobody went crazy. Marshawn Lynch, who has been in the league for the past eleven years, never stood for the national anthem; nobody went crazy or found that disrespectful.

However, Colin Kaepernick took a knee, and everyone found that very disrespectful. Some say it would've been alright if he hadn't been verbal about why he did what he did. But many of us tend to miss the big picture. It wasn't Kaepernick's idea to take a knee, someone else who was in the military told Kaepernick the best way to respect the military is to take a knee, and that person's name is Nate Boyer. Nate Boyer, was a former long snapper in the NFL, served in the military for six years with multiple tours in Iraq and Afghanistan. This veteran was the individual who told Kaepernick about taking a knee. Mr. Boyer told him this is how you honor the vets who served the military.

This is what Mr. Boyer said when he was interviewed with NPR (National Public Radio), *"How did you get to talk with Colin Kaepernick, to begin with? How did your conversation ensue?"*

Boyer's response was, *"You know, this was two years ago, 2016 during the preseason. And he, you know, had sat on the bench. And I think it was his third time he'd sat on the bench. But it was the first time it had received national attention. And, you know, he got questioned about it, and he said, well, I'm not going to stand for the flag of a country that oppresses black people and people of color. And then he talked about, you know, social injustices and police brutality and why he thought, you know, he shouldn't be standing for the anthem. And it struck a chord with me, of course, and it struck a chord with a lot of people - a lot of people in the veteran community as well - because obviously the flag and the anthem and what that stuff stands for means something, you know, very different to us. And I was pretty upset, you know, just because I felt like he didn't understand what those symbols really represent. And - but instead of letting my anger overwhelm me, I decided to relax a little bit, and I wrote this open letter that was just explaining my experiences, my relationship to the flag. And Colin actually reached out, said he wanted to meet with me. And we sat in the lobby of the team hotel, discussed our situation, our different opinions and feelings about all this. And I suggested him taking a knee instead of sitting even though I wanted him to stand, and he wanted to sit. And it was, like, this compromise that we sort of came to. And that's where the kneeling began."* Many assumed that it was Kaepernick's idea to take a knee.

We may not understand the "why" behind people's actions, and we may not understand the differences. Still, in order for us to really understand the purpose behind why someone is doing something, we have to be willing to be open-minded and have an open heart to receive what someone is telling us.

The interview proceeded, and Boyer was asked, *"How did the idea of taking a knee come to you?* Boyer's response was, *"I thought - at that time I said, look, I think your point has definitely been made that everyone's listening. Like, let's make a plan of attack now. And, you know, let's work on action for it. But he said, you know, what I've committed to this, and - I'm not going to do it*

until I start to see these changes I want to see. And, you know, I respected that decision and opinion. And I thought kneeling - personally, so I don't speak for everybody, I don't speak for every veteran. I've been told that numerous times by many people. But I thought kneeling was more respectful, and I will say that being alongside his teammates was the biggest thing for me. And, you know, people - in my opinion and in my experience, kneeling's never been in our history really seen as a disrespectful act. I mean, people kneel when they get knighted. You kneel to propose to your wife, and you take a knee to pray. And soldiers often take a knee in front of a fallen brother's grave to pay respects. So, I thought, if anything, besides standing, that was the most respectful. But, of course, that's just my opinion…"
(https://www.npr.org/the-veteran-and-nfl-player-who-advised-kaepernick-to-take-a-knee).

Taking a knee is more than just police brutality. Taking a knee has to do with every system in America that does not benefit every citizen in America.

How do we say it's for the people and by the people but then mistreat certain groups of people? How do we say that we, as a nation, live up to the constitution, but when black and brown people are using their constitutional rights, it's considered unconstitutional? If we are not willing to stand for justice for all, then why do we pledge justice for all? Malcolm X once said, *"I believe that there will ultimately be a clash between the oppressed and those that do the oppressing. I believe that there will be a clash between those who want freedom, justice, and equality for everyone and those who want to continue the systems of exploitation."*

Kaepernick used his platform to attack systematic oppression; it inspired many people throughout the nation to take a knee and stand for justice in America. Everyone began taking a knee. I believe that Kaepernick taking a knee was a wake-up call so America could see the truth that was already clear. Kaepernick explained why he took a knee and why he's not going to give up on something that he started.

On April 21, 2018, Kaepernick was giving a speech in Amsterdam at the Amnesty International Ambassador of Conscience on why he took a knee while receiving the *"Ambassador of Conscience awards."* During his speech, he said, *"People sometimes forget that love is at the root of our resistance."* He continued and said, *"My love for my people serves as the fuel that motivates me and fortifies me on my mission. It is the people's unbroken love for themselves that motivates me even when faced with dehumanizing norms of a system that can lead to the loss of one's life over simply being black. History has proven that there has never been a period in the history of America where anti-blackness has not been an ever-present terror. Racialized oppression and dehumanization are woven into the very fabric of our nation. The effects of which can be seen in the lawful lynching of the black and brown people by the police. And the mass incarceration of black and brown lives in the prison industrial complex. While America builds itself as the land of the free, the receipts show that the U.S has incarcerated approximately 2.2 million people, the largest prison population in the history of humankind. As Police officers continue to terrorize black and brown communities, abusing their power and then hiding behind their blue wall of silence, the law allows them to kill us with virtual impunity.*

I have realized that love, that sometimes manifests itself as black rage, is a beautiful form of defiance against a system that seeks to suppress our humanity, a system that wants us to hate ourselves. But I remind you, it is love that is at the root of our resistance. It is our love for 12-year-old Tamir Rice, who was gunned down by the police in less than two seconds that will not allow us to bury our anger. It is our love for Philando Castile, who was executed in front of his partner and his daughter that keeps us fighting back. It is our love for Stephon Clark, who was lynched in his grandma's backyard that will not allow us to stop until we liberate our people. Our love is not an individualized love; it is a collective love. A collective love that is constantly combatting forms of racialized hate. Chattel Slavery, Jim Crow, new Jim Crow, massive plantations, mass incarceration, slave patrols, and police patrols. We, as a collective, since the colonization of the Americas, have been combatting collective forms of systematic, racialized hate and oppression.

But I am hopeful and inspired. This is why we have to protest; this is why we are so passionate. We protest because we love ourselves, and we love our people. It was James Baldwin who said, to be black in America and to be relatively conscious, is to be in a rage almost all the time. My question is: Why aren't all people? How can you stand for the national anthem of a nation that preaches and propagates freedom and justice for all, that is so unjust to so many of the people living there? How can you not be in a rage when you know you are always at risk of death in the streets, or enslavement in the prison system? How can you willingly be blind to the truth of systemic racialized injustice?

When Malcolm X said, "*I'm for truth, no matter who tells it. I'm for justice, no matter who it's for or against. I'm a human being first and foremost. And as such, I am for whoever, and whatever benefits humanity as a whole.*" *I took that to heart. While taking a knee is a physical display that challenges the merits of who is excluded from the notion of freedom, liberty, and justice for all. The protest is also rooted in the convergence of my moralistic beliefs and my love for the people. Seeking the truth, finding the truth, telling the truth, and living the truth, has been, and always will be what guides my actions. For as long as I have a beating heart, I will continue to work on this path on behalf of the people.*"
(https://youtu.be/5B8VU3Jykvl)

I remember showing the video clip to people who were not of color; I informed the audience to really have the heart to receive and listen. The audience saw the clip, but they still missed the bigger picture from the clip. They were so tuned into what he did, that they didn't want to listen to the "why." They were so focused on believing that it was disrespectful to take a knee that they failed to understand the reason for the fight.

I wanted them to understand my position as a Haitian American man. If we really understood anything about the Haitian Revolution and the fight that the Haitians had to endure just to gain independence, then they would understand, but they didn't. I began to give different examples of how discrimination has affected me. I remember going on and on with the audience and sharing stories that they never had to encounter or even experience. One of the people in the audience asked, how did that happen? I looked at every white person in the eye, and I told them, "It happens because the system doesn't benefit me. The system was not created for me. The system was designed for you and you are benefiting very well from this system. It was created to see you elevate and to see the black and brown people stay at a neutral level. Kaepernick opened the eyes of America so America could see what they don't want to face."

John Pavlovitz, who is an American Christian pastor, known for his social and political writings from a liberal Christian perspective, said, "*Colin Kaepernick was right about us, white America. He was right to kneel because when he did, he fully exposed us. He exposed us as we became viscerally disgusted, not by the reckless disregard of black lives, but by the earnest and open declaration of black grief at their premature passing. He exposed us when we felt it was our right to tell another human being how to express their personal freedoms, during an anthem supposedly devoted to celebrating those personal freedoms.*

He exposed us when we treasured flags and songs over flesh and blood; when we repeatedly ignored dissenting facts in order to hold on to our easy and lazy outrage. He exposed us when we chose to listen to the words of a divisive white President over athletes of color, as to their motives and intentions. He exposed us as we had the stratospheric nerve to lecture him about the right way for him to protest as a citizen of this country.

He exposed us when we chastised him for the manner in which he expressed his freedom, because it was a little too "free" for us. He exposed us as we saw all of these things, and still remained silent. And he's exposing us now, those of us who are burning shoes and cutting up socks and boycotting Nike—because a strong man of color who will not be shamed into silence or allow us to make the rules, still makes our blood boil—which is the most telling and tragic truth of all.

Privilege is a terrible disease, because it is invisible to those most fully afflicted with it. When most deeply in the throes of the heart sickness, they cannot see themselves, or the reality of the moment. They do not require data to be disgusted or truth to craft the narrative of their suffering. They simply feel fear, even when it is unfounded; oppression, even when there is none; offensive, even when they have no cause.

If you're seething right now, this is a symptom. If you're still doubling down on some imagined defense of "America" while simultaneously seeking to deny people of color America's most elemental liberties—you're proving Colin Kaepernick right. If you're still refusing to believe the player's voices over the one in your head or in a President's tweets or in an angry country singer's rants—you're showing why Kaepernick was correct to protest from the very beginning. You're confirming the very reason his knee first hit the turf two-year ago: because too many white people want to go through life undisturbed by any reality of their advantages.

They will do anything not to be inconvenienced by the ugly realities of a system that they are the greatest beneficiaries of. They will be profoundly pissed off when a person of color intrudes on their entertainment with a dose of sobering truth about life and death. They will follow the most convoluted, nonsensical thought lines, if this allows them to quiet marginalized people and to evade culpability for their own prejudices toward those marginalized people. It isn't surprising that the folks so violently shaken by Colin Kaepernick, profess to defend a freedom they don't like him exercising. They're the same ones saying that they love both America—and a draft-dodging, Russian-beholden, POW-belittling President. They're the same people who say they want to rewind and reclaim America's "greatness", while ignoring how much suffering and injustice that supposed greatness created for so many. They're the same people who claim allegiance to both Jesus and to Donald Trump. Cognitive dissonance doesn't register when you're white and terrified of losing your dominance.

By kneeling, Colin Kaepernick let us do the work for him. He didn't need to belabor the point, he just let us show ourselves. He allowed white America's responses to reveal who we are. He saw something ugly in us that we didn't and still don't want to see."

https://johnpavlovitz.com/2018/09/04/colin-kaepernick-was-right-about-us/?

We pledge for justice
but don't serve it
We pledge for liberty yet
don't provide it
We pledge for freedom
but don't serve it
We say all men are created equal
but it's not apparent
We tell officers to take an oath in front of the public
but yet they keep their jobs when evidence of injustice
arises
We pledge for solidarity
but it's not evident
We say it's for the people and by the people
but we can't tell
We pledge for unity

yet don't show it
We pledge for equality
yet; equality is rarely found
We pledge for many things
but yet don't show it

As a country, we are good at babbling words and talking, but we don't turn those words into action. The truth is the truth, even if you don't like it. Just because you're not affected by something does not mean it's not affecting someone else. To many times we tell people *"this is a safe place, what is said here, stay here"* but when the individual is sharing their hurts, their pains, their fears, we tend to silence them because we don't want to hear it. We tend to act like we care, but deep inside we don't.

At what point will every citizen benefit from being a citizen? When will America really care for justice, equality, and liberty? America ignores when a police officer kills a person of color, and nothing is done about it.

A Virginia police officer got fired for refusing to shoot a black man. The system that is built in America never gave people of color an opportunity for justice, but then get mad that Kaepernick is taking a knee. If you are mad that someone is speaking up and fighting back because of the injustice in America, then you are part of the problem!

The next time you see someone taking a knee, don't be quick to judge- stand next to them. If you want to know why they are taking a knee, ask them and be willing to listen. Being privileged is so deep that it blinds people to really see the struggles that someone else endures and because it does not affect them, they will turn a blind eye to the situation.

Within law enforcement, there is something that is called *"The blue wall of silence, blue code, and blue shield."* These are terms used in the United States to designate the formal rule that exists among police officers to not report colleagues' errors, misconducts, or crimes, including police brutality. If an officer sees a colleague do something unjust, they cannot report it because, if they do, they are considered a betrayer in the force. Because of the codes, many officers abuse their authority and still stay in the force with pay on administrative leave. However, some officers who do their jobs honestly lose their jobs.

One incident that some of us may recall is the incident that happened in 2016, where a former police officer in Weirton, West Virginia, got fired for not shooting a black suspect. Officer Mader was the first responding officer to a call regarding a 23-year-old RJ Williams believed to be suicidal. The officer who is white, made a determination that Williams didn't pose as a threat to him or fellow officers even though Williams was holding a gun. Mader told the guardian news reporter that Williams wasn't aggressive. *"He didn't seem in position to want to use a gun against anybody. He never pointed it at me. I de-escalated a situation and was fired for doing my duty to protect and to serve and not shoot first."*

Why should one be penalized if they are doing the right thing? Why should one still hold a badge when they are doing the wrong thing?

Weeks after the termination of Mader, he was called a "coward" by his colleagues because he decided not to use deadly force on the suspect. Mader told ProPublica, which is an independent, nonprofit newsroom that produces investigative journalism with a moral authority that he was trying to calm Williams down. Mader said, *"It was really just talking to him like he was a human being talk to him like a guy who was in a wrong state of mind, like a guy who needed to be calmed down, who needed help. I didn't want to shoot him,"* Mader added. *"I don't want to say this, because it's really corny, but I was kind of sacrificing my well-being for him."*

There are many officers who have spoken out about other officers' actions and got fired for reporting the effects of another officer. These days, even if one does not say it, video reports it, and even with the video, the crimes still get justified because it's black or brown life, while the video clearly shows injustice from the beginning to the end. Why not take a knee? Why not stand for justice? Why not stand for equality for everyone?

Purpose Behind the Movement- Schools

We tend to tell people that education is the key to success, but minority students don't get the same access to quality education because of the color of their skin. As someone who goes into the schools to mentor kids, there's a significant racial tension in the schools that has not been addressed. Within the school systems, there's a disparity in education that educators won't talk about because they will have to buck up against a system that was not designed for children of color to succeed in the first place.

The biggest disparities in education is race. An article called "*Failing Black Boys*," written by Hildebrand Pelzer III, who was a former principal of a Philadelphia public school says, "*The rate of school suspensions has doubled in the last decade or so, most dramatically for students of color. In fact, the Education Department's Office for Civil Rights says black students are three times more likely to be suspended or expelled—even as young as preschool. Meanwhile, a large-scale study out of Texas found that students who were suspended or expelled were three times more likely to encounter the juvenile justice system than those who stayed in school—a direct link in the schools-to-prison pipeline.*"
(www.thephiladelphiacitizen.org/failing-black-boys)

I have witnessed how teachers treat kids who are black, and brown compared to those who are white. A white kid can misbehave, and his/her behavior will be justified. A black kid with the same bad behavior will be punished immediately.

The majority of teachers that are teaching our black and brown kids are not even certified to teach. According to the Department of Education, *"High-poverty schools had higher percentages, on average, of teachers who were not fully certified than schools with lower poverty rates."* There you have it. The fact that our education system is built to see our black and brown kids fail is unacceptable. The Department of Education knows that there are teachers out there teaching our kids with no credentials. There are disparities in the achievement and opportunity gaps for children of color. If every child doesn't have the same opportunity, how can we talk about closing out a gap of achievement? *Martin Luther King Jr. once said, "Injustice anywhere is a threat to justice everywhere."*

I remember when I was in the K-12 public school system, and educators told me to give up and throw in the towel, they were trying to plant seeds of failure in my mind. I used their negative words to prove them wrong! We tend to say that our kids are the leaders of tomorrow but then fail to give them the resources that they need to become the great leaders in their communities, schools, and wherever they may go. Have you ever wondered why our schools are diverse, but our staff is not? Have you ever wondered why there's a lack of representation in our schools?

According to the article, *"The Burden of Being a Black Teacher,"* written by Emily Deruy who was a former staff writer at the Atlantic, where she covered education said, *"Only 7 percent of the country's teachers are black although African Americans make up around 16 percent of the overall student population."* Mrs. Deruy went further and stated that government data from the 2012 Schools and Staffing survey showed that many black teachers experience constant tension at work between a sense of frustration at being "pigeonholed" into teaching primarily black students. Deruy went on and said, *"If some black teachers feel like their colleagues think they're only good enough for black students, does that imply those colleagues also think black students deserve less than other students? Does that suggest black teachers' and white colleagues see them as less qualified? Does that indicate white teachers won't do as much to support black students as they will to help other students? These questions are difficult to answer because the report features the perceptions of black teachers and not white teachers. But the perceptions of these black teachers are valuable regardless of what white teachers think because they inform who stays in the profession and who leaves."*

If you are going to be a teacher, you have to be willing to treat the kids you are teaching with love and respect, and it shouldn't matter what the child's skin color is. It shouldn't matter the background of the child because every child has the potential to be whatever they want to be. The question that educators have to ask themselves is, *"Do I believe that this kid can become great? Or do I not think that they can become great because of their background and the color of their skin?"* We need to have justice across the board in education. There are many teachers in our schools that run away from authenticity, and they fail to realize that being authentic and real is the best way to get to someone's heart.

I believe I have a different impact and reach when it comes to students of color because I am a black man. I can reach these students in a way most white teachers can't. The reason being is I can relate to their struggle. I had a job as a program manager at an elementary in Sea-Tac, WA, where I was the person in charge of the after-school program. The teachers told me about the kids who they were having a hard time dealing with. They informed me that I would have a hard time with these kids. With confidence, I told the teachers it wouldn't be that way with me. I remember this day as if it was yesterday, there were kids lined up for the after-school program I shook each of those kids' hand and introduced myself. By the time I got back to the front of the line, the black and brown kids were smiling and rejoicing. One of the teachers witnessed what happened, and she came up to me and told me, *"I never seen any of these kids smiling and happy to be a part of the after-school program. What did you do to make all these kids smile?"* I told the teacher that I didn't do anything but connect with each of them individually. That and the fact they were probably excited to see a black male teach.

Throughout the years in my field, I always hear people say, *"Why don't more black and brown people become teachers? How come the blacks and browns are not being represented in the schools?"* If we understand the system that has been built in education from the beginning to the end, we will then understand why there are not enough black and brown teachers in our schools. Study shows that black students who have teachers who look like them have higher test scores than white students and will be motivated to go to college and finish. The educational system has always suppressed a healthy learning environment for children of color; kids grow up to be adults, and adults remember the system that broke them. Could this be one of the reasons why blacks don't teach?

A study that was done at Johns Hopkins University found that when a white teacher and a black teacher consider the same black student, the white teacher is 30% less likely to think the student will graduate from a four-year college. White teachers, the researchers also found, are nearly 40% less likely to think their black students will graduate from high school. The expectation that the teachers have for black students are so low, it's embarrassing. Teachers, why don't you give your all to the black students like you do to the white students? Teachers, why don't you treat these kids with the same treatment you treat the white kids? Teachers, what is it about the black child that makes you believe these students can't become successful? What is it about the black child that makes you think that the student will become a product of their environment and nothing better? If you are a teacher or someone who works in the education field, and you believe that someone's success is defined by how they look, then you need to resign. If you believe that the color of someone's skin will determine the route they will take in life, then you need to resign!

I remember being asked to be a keynote speaker at an event for professional development for educators. I did something that I have never done, and I told the organizer at this educational event not to put a picture of me on the flyer and not to mention anything about my skin color but let my introduction speak for itself.

I remember being in the back, getting mentally ready to go on the stage. I was eager to see the audience's facial expression once they heard my introduction. When the organizer was done speaking, I walk slowly towards the stage, and I heard clapping all around the room. The claps are getting louder and louder to the point where I couldn't help but speed walk towards the stage. The moment I got on the stage, the clapping stopped, and mouths start to drop, people are scratching their heads as if they were confused about something. Based on their expressions, I could tell they didn't think that a man of color was going to be the one teaching on professional development. I asked them what they expected. After hearing some of the derogatory remarks coming from these educators, I then responded with, *"This is what you do when you go to your classes and teach kids."* The room became silent, and eyes got all big as if they were hit with some deep conviction because they knew deep inside that is the truth. The topic that I was talking about was, "giving your all no matter what." What they were doing was responding in a way that was not welcoming because of their negative perception of brown and black people.

Many educators are running on E (empty), and they think that they are running on F (Full) because they have planned for the academic week. Somewhere, before these teachers became teachers, they were taught how to hate people who were different from them. They were instructed to believe that a particular group of people were less.

Nelson Mandela once said, *"No one is born hating another person because of the color of his skin, or his background, or his religion. People must learn to hate, and if they can learn to hate, they can be taught to love, for love comes more naturally to the human heart than its opposite."* When love is not in the center, hate will activate. When love is not in the center, segregation will be active.

While I'm speaking, I can see that I am reaching their hearts, black, brown, and white people begin to get up and hug each other with tears in their eyes. When you hear *"Black Lives Matter,"* understand that this is a chant for every system in America to change and not just law enforcement.

Statistics

One of my good friends, Charles Dickerson, conducted a survey in 2016, surveying middle school and high school kids from different school districts. Dickerson had an opportunity to talk about how the atmosphere and the shaping of a school can determine what goes through the kid's mind while being in the class. Dickerson always says, "*Just because you're filling a seat does not make you a student in the seat.*"

In the survey, the students were given two questions to answer honestly. They didn't have to put their names down, but they did have to state what race they identify as. The first question that was on the paper was, "Do you feel comfortable when the police walk through your schools? If yes, why and if no, why?" For middle school students, 60% of the white students said yes, they feel safe. The other 40% of the white students don't feel safe because they don't understand why the police are in the schools when there are no calls that were made for them to be in the schools. And 75% of the students of color in the middle school said they don't feel safe because it's as if the police are watching them even when they are not doing anything wrong. Some of them said they know the police are in the schools for them because their brothers or sisters were a part of the system and they believe that the schools believe that they will be a part of the system too. Another 15% of the students of color said they have no reason not to feel safe, especially when they are just minding their own business and staying out of trouble.

When the high school kids answered the questions, 50% of the white students said yes, they feel safe because their skin color is not a threat to the society. While the other 50% of the white students said they don't feel safe because their peers don't feel safe when encountering law enforcement. One of the students said, *"If the people that I love don't feel safe, how can I feel safe when the people that I love have a piece of my heart? So, how can I shower in safety if the people who are in my heart are not showered in the same safety?"* Anonymous.

While 35% of the students of color in these different school district say they don't feel harm when they see law enforcement, they still are cautious and aware of what could happen to them because their parents informed them that their skin color is a threat to law enforcement. Then 65% of students of color in the high schools say they get shaken up anytime they see a man with a badge looking at them because they feel like they are after them. They were also asked these questions: *Before your school was rebuilt, how was the atmosphere?*

Since your school is now rebuilt, how is the atmosphere? The middle school students didn't feel like they had a say about how the school was built, but one thing they said was that the schools needed to have better food. This response was the same response that the high school students had.

The mentality that the middle and high school kids had was to just go to school, do work and get good grades. The students said they didn't pay much attention to the atmosphere but what they paid attention to was the lack of care that teachers had for the students of color. In middle schools, 60% of the white kids said they see that the school is bigger, but it does not seem welcoming for every student. One white student said, *"The school looks like the jail that I go to visit my brother and, every time when I walk down the halls to go to my classes, it's as if I am about to step into my brother's hallway to go into his jail cell." Anonymous.* While other white students in middle school said, it's good that it's bigger but to make it better, we need more teachers that care for every student and not just for me or the kids who are white. While 80% of the students of color felt like the school was reminding them that prison was their only future. One student of color said, *"The school looks like the score jail that my church goes and visits every month. In the score jail, the inmates look like me so when I am walking through my school, I really feel like the school district rebuilt it to give a message to students of color. The school is shaped like a jail facility, and the stairs are set up is the same way." Anonymous.*

The other 20% of students of color in the middle school said it's good that it's bigger but the problem is that the teachers can't connect to every student the way they want to connect to every student. One student said, *"I know the heart of my teacher and it bothers her that she can't reach us the way she wants to reach us because the school is bigger which means the classes are larger. Some kids will not get the attention they need. When the school was smaller, my teacher connected to every student and every student in her classroom felt like they were valued, loved, and appreciated. But now, since the school is big, the students don't get that same attention." Anonymous.* Of the white students 75% said they are

91

walking through a jail facility and 15% of the white students said the rebuilding does not affect them but it affects the students who don't look like them and maybe this is a way for America to profit from the school-to-prison pipeline.

One students said, *"I remember pulling up to the school and my parents and I cried because the school was looking like a federal jail facility. It touched my heart because the school to prison pipeline is so real that it targets the students of color. And we can't say there's no child left behind when we are creating a setting where children are being left behind. You have the black and brown kids who are being left behind every single year in the education system. These kids could be kids with special needs, or just regular kids in the school. But because their skin color is black or brown, they are not being seen as a valuable, so, instead, the district agrees to rebuild schools that look like a youth jail. Just because my friends who are black and brown are not being lynched does not mean that mentally they are not being lynched. Freedom does not start because there's no shackles on someone's feet or hand, freedom starts in the mind, and if the mind is not free, then freedom will always be a fight. So, if I can see the school looking like a jail and being built like a jail, I could just imagine how my black and brown friends feel and the imagery that goes through their minds while walking through the hallways."* Anonymous.

And 45% of the students of color said they don't understand why the school was rebuilt because ever since it got rebuilt the atmosphere felt like it was dark.

One student said, *you can't build a house without a solid foundation and I believe that's what happened in my school. My school doesn't have a solid foundation. And when I say foundation, I am not referring to people who are graduating and moving up to the next chapter of life. But I am referring to our textbooks, the lack of diversity that is in our staff that does not represent every student body. Before money was spent on building a new building it should have been spent in investing in the lives of us children because they say we are the next future leaders in America. But how can we be the next future leaders in America if our lives are not being invested in especially in education?" Anonymous.*

I remember seeing these numbers and, when having lunch with Mr. Dickerson, all I could do was shed tears. These are the voices of students from every walk of life and from different school districts, they pretty much all think the same thing.

The moment I saw Federal Way High School in Federal Way, WA being built, I automatically said out loud that this looks like a jail. I saw police cars parked on the grass overnight. It didn't sit with me well so, what I did, I took a step higher and reached out to Mike Pellicciotti who is an attorney and also a Washington State Representative representing the 30th legislative district, an area that includes Federal Way, Algona, Auburn, Pacific, Milton, and Des Moines.

I met Pellicciotti through an event at a church in Tacoma, WA, where I had the opportunity to talk about issues that deal with mass incarceration. Within that event there was a campaign group that was there to get signatures to bring this issue of mass incarceration to Olympia WA. While being there, others and I brought the issue to Pellicciotti regarding the schools looking like jails and we were trying to figure out why.

Pellicciotti was new, and he was just serving his first term however, he was listening to the people. He didn't have the answers then, but he informed everyone that his door was open and he was willing to meet and talk with people. After talking with him, it hit me like a ton of bricks, were other schools being rebuilt to look like prisons?

When I looked further into this, I realized this is part of the school-to-prison pipeline that was designed to target areas of poverty and people of color. It starts with creating the image, then the atmosphere, not investing in the students, and the end result will be kids in the judicial system. This is the school-to-prison pipeline.

Anytime there's lack of investment in someone's life, something horrific is going to take place. Teachers have these students more often than their parents have them. If we invested in every child, then the results would be higher graduation rates, lower numbers of students being incarcerated, and the school-to-prison pipeline ratio would drop significantly.

When I heard Kaepernick's "why" on taking a knee, I thought about the survey that Dickerson did; I put the puzzle together and realized that we all must take a knee.

CHAPTER FIVE

MY STORY

Imagine a child coming to America to go to school and English is his second language. A child who was born in the Caribbean, in the islands of Haiti and his parents finding out that he has epilepsy. A young boy at three months old being diagnosed with this condition, his family realizes that this child can't be left alone because of the seizures that can take place anywhere at any time.

Jean-Pierre's beginning stages of life represented a time of uncertainty, not knowing if today would be the last day or if he would have more time in this world. Growing up for Jean-Pierre wasn't easy. It was a tough childhood that led to young adulthood. There were battles he faced at a young age where he had to fight the good fight to overcome the obstacles that he eventually overcame. Going through school, Jean-Pierre fell in a category of Special Ed and had an IEP (Individual

Education Plan) throughout his K-12 schooling. For the first four years in school, he had an interpreter, he also took ESL classes to learn the English language. He was a kid with special needs and the teachers did not know how to deal with him.

Jean-Pierre had all odds against him. People thought he would be a statistic, just another black child who wouldn't make it. Jean-Pierre didn't know how to get along with others well; he had anger issues and he couldn't retain information that was given to him. What a lot of people didn't know about Jean-Pierre was that his brain didn't work well together. If his right brain was working, his left brain wouldn't be working and vice versa. Jean-Pierre was a brilliant young man but because of a deep father wounds, he found himself hurting other people because he was hurt. He eventually found himself getting in tons of trouble due to his actions he chose to take, eventually, people around him had concerns about the wellbeing of this child. The concerns came from the staff in the schools and volunteers.

The staff and volunteers didn't understand what was going on but they knew if nothing changes, then Jean-Pierre could go the wrong direction in life. Jean-Pierre had hopes he was going to be somebody and knew that he could do great things, but because of the lack of support, he wasn't able to see that. Jean-Pierre found himself calling out to God in the 8th grade praying for a mentor to come his way. He knew that high school would be very challenging and he recognized that a mentor was what he needed to walk this journey of life so he wouldn't be a statistic.

He believed that God would give him a mentor that would invest in him and would be right beside him all the way. Months passed and no mentor was in sight. However, he kept on persevering and believing in God. Eventually, someone by the name of Rashad Norris showed up in Jean-Pierre's life and helped him.

There was still some internal pain that Jean-Pierre never talked about or dealt with that carried over into his high school career. In high school, he became the kid who was full of drama and involved in toxic relationships because of the pain he was dealing with. Educators had given up on this child.

He believed that, one day, he would become a motivational speaker, an author, and someone who is an advocate for kids with disabilities and kids of color. Jean-Pierre knew that there had to be a bigger reason why he was going through what he was going through, and with the help of his mentor; he triumphed over pain.

Even when Jean-Pierre shared his dreams and passions with peers and educators, they all laughed at him and told him that it would never be possible. Peers and educators questioned his belief on why he thought the dreams he had would be achieved. He felt hopeless at times.

Through the help of his mentor, Mr. Norris, Jean-Pierre knew that if his mentor could do it, then he could too. If you asked Jean-Pierre what made him not give up on life, he would tell you MLK and Mr. Norris because these two individuals gave him hope because they looked like him and since he saw two influential people who looked like him, he gained confidence and believed he could be influential himself.

Jean-Pierre found himself in high school writing and declaring in the atmosphere what he wanted. Around his senior year in high school, he found himself shocking educators and peers with a big achievement.

On October 13th-16th of 2010, Jean-Pierre had an opportunity to travel to Kansas City Missouri, to speak at a national conference called ASHA (American School Health Association), speaking about kids with special needs. He was sharing his own story of being someone with special needs. Months later, he found himself being the keynote speaker for the 20th year anniversary of the City of Sea-Tac, located in WA . He was also an advocate for students at Highline College in Des Moines WA. He found himself achieving two milestones that he wrote and declared in the atmosphere that manifested in front of his eyes.

While at Highline, Jean-Pierre received the award, *"The Most Inspirational Student Award,"* by the Trio Department on the college campus. The award he received wasn't nominated by staff and faculty but it was nominated by other students on campus that believed that he deserved the award. While working as a student ambassador, he also got awarded the student employee of the year for his department.

Through poetry, Jean-Pierre expresses his message for justice that brings imagery, emotions and heart-felt reactions from the audience. While being a strong activist and giving back to the community Jean-Pierre found himself having his own negative interaction with law enforcement.

On August 24th-26th he went camping in Cowlitz Campground in WA. Jean-Pierre was on state route seven going 25 MPH and was using his Waze App for GPS because it also tracks the speed. When he looked into his rear-view mirror, he saw a car turning into State route seven with lights on and, because of that, he pulled over so the vehicle could pass. The passenger in the seat was kind of confused why Jean-Pierre was pulling over.

All of a sudden, Jean-Pierre and Jerrell noticed that the police was pulling them over but they didn't know why they were being pulled over. As the officer approached the vehicle, he struck his taillight on the driver side with the palm of his hands and proceeded to inform them that he was with the Sheriff's office and was wondering if Jean-Pierre knew why he was being pulled over. Jean-Pierre stated that he was not sure why he got pulled over because he was going the speed limit. The officer chuckled and stated that Jean-Pierre's speedometer must be broken because he clocked him going 40 MPH in a 25 MPH zone.

He was in shock because his speedometer showed something other than what the officer stated. Jean-Pierre had his documents ready for the officer before the officer approached his window. The officer started asking Jean-Pierre & Jerrell what they were doing on this side of town. Jean-Pierre responded and let the officer know that they went camping over the weekend with some people from their church. The officer then went to his vehicle with Jean-Pierre's docs and shortly came back and informed Jean-Pierre that there was a no-contact order in place. Jean-Pierre let the officer know that he had the wrong individual because he had no knowledge what the officer was talking about.

At this point, he began to feel fearful for his life and agitated because this was the first time he heard this and not sure where it came from. Jean-Pierre asked the officer if he was sure this no-contact order was him. The officer then stated that someone by the name of Josie placed a no-contact order against him. Because of this false accusation of a no-contact order in place, the officer then proceeded to ask the passenger for his ID and stated that he was not going to put him in the system but just wanted to verify if he was Josie because, if he was, then Jean-Pierre could get into trouble.

Proceeding with caution, Jerrell let the officer know that his ID was in the backseat in his bag and needs to reach for it to give it to him. Jerrell told the officer that he is going to reach for his ID in the backseat and asked if that was okay. After saying it multiple times, the officer didn't respond which led Jean-Pierre to raise his voice and tell the officer that the passenger is going to go to the backseat to get his ID; he asked louder if that was okay.

The officer said okay and immediately placed his hands on his gun shaking it on the side of his hip. Because of that action, they became even more fearful for their life. They wondered if they were going to die. The officer looked at the ID and returned it to the passenger. Jean-Pierre then proceeded to ask the officer how he would have knowledge if someone placed a no-contact order against him? The officer replied that Jean-Pierre should have been served papers. The officer then walked off.

When the officer came back to Jean-Pierre's vehicle, the officer said that it was the wrong person and the birthdate was different. The birthdate was one day off on the 20th and not the 21st. Again, Jean-Pierre questioned in his head, how someone could put his license number in the system and someone have the same name and address as him but the birthdate be different. Jean-Pierre knew the officer was lying because when he asked the officer, he started stuttering; he was caught abusing his authority.

Eventually, Jean-Pierre met an individual by the name of John Bunn who was wrongfully accused of a crime that he never committed. Mr. Bunn was telling his story which inspired Jean-Pierre to show Bunn the letter of the courts of how he was wrongfully accused of a crime that he never committed.

When this incident happened, Jean-Pierre reached out to his good friend, Kris Wilburn, to see if he was willing to drive two hours down to a city to fight this ticket in court. Mr. Wilburn and Jean-Pierre drove down to go to the court room and fight this ticket that Jean-Pierre received. While being in the courtroom, Jean-Pierre gave the judge his side of what happen and the case was dismissed because the police officer statement didn't line up. The ticket happened in Morton County but the statement said Chehalis WA. Jean-Pierre's height on the statement said 5'0 but Jean-Pierre's actual height is 5'8. Because of the statement not lining up, the judge dismissed the case because of the police statement and for wrongfully accusing Jean-Pierre of a crime that was never committed. Because of this event, he became a member of the Seattle chapter of the NAACP fighting a fight for justice and police accountability.

Jean-Pierre's why is to empower a generation, equip them with tools and strategies to overcome obstacles and bounce back from any setbacks that they have endured. Today, Jean-Pierre runs a mentor group that equips young men of color with strategies and tools to walk into their full potential.

Josias' setbacks have given hope and encouragement to many people, from different aspects of life to be an overcomer and fight the good fight. If your why doesn't make you cry, you have to evaluate your why. Whatever your why is, make sure that love is in the center because that is what will bring change.

Made in the USA
Middletown, DE
12 October 2021